DOES MY SOUL LOOK BIG IN THIS?

Rosemary Lain-Priestley

To Lizzy,

With best wishes

+ blessings

Rosemary

... and from Kyra
to a friend who has
a very 'big soul'!
K x

SPCK

First published in Great Britain in 2012

Society for Promoting Christian Knowledge
36 Causton Street
London SW1P 4ST
www.spckpublishing.co.uk

British Library Cataloguing-in-Publication Data
A catalogue record for this book is available from the British Library

ISBN 978–0–281–06368–0
eBook ISBN 978–0–281–06855–5

Typeset by Graphicraft Ltd, Hong Kong
First printed in Great Britain by Ashford Colour Press
Subsequently digitally printed in Great Britain

Produced on paper from sustainable forests

For my female clergy colleagues in
the Church of England,
who for twenty-five years have nurtured souls
with imagination, grace and courage

Contents

Acknowledgements

A book of this nature becomes entwined with the author's life: the book gets caught up in the life and the life gets caught up in the book. While I wrote about growing our souls I was searching for a better sense and understanding of my own. Which is probably why several deadlines passed by. And why I owe some people particular thanks for the part they played, during this year of writing, in shaping the book and nurturing my soul.

My love and thanks go to:

Paula Gooder, for expanding my soul with the sort of theology that engages with life as real people live it; also for reading several chapters at very short notice and suggesting invaluable connections and changes.

Kyra Sheppard, for willingly and cheerfully making *Does my Soul* her holiday reading; for perceptive and encouraging feedback; and, in another role, for being an inspiring teacher to our children.

Debra Deaville, for patience, sensitivity, wisdom and skill in enabling me to unfold the second half of life.

Alison Barr at SPCK, for believing that there was a third book in me, for knowing that the first draft was not it, and for giving me the confidence and motivation to discover what I really wanted to say.

Ali Lyon, for a year's worth of discussions over curry as to what the book was and should be about; for countless insights into the nature of a soul-full life; for patient reading and rereading of the entire book; and for the sort of friendship that makes life continually fascinating.

And, as ever, to Antony Lain, for unparalleled patience when for weeks on end I worked into the early hours; for making it possible for me to pursue the activities that enliven my soul; and for 17 years of exploring life together with love, passion and humour.

Introduction

This is a book about the big questions in life; those that on some level nag away at most of us. We may all have different versions of them, but they will probably look something like this: *Does my life have a point? Do things really have to change? Am I happy enough? Where on earth is home? Will I ever be 'in' with the 'in crowd'? Is there never time to breathe?* At first sight these questions may seem a bit random and disconnected. However, their interdependence will become apparent as they unfold through the chapters that follow and as we come to see why each in turn has the potential to grow our soul.

For a lot of people these issues become particularly insistent in mid-life. However, they can surface at any time and for many different reasons. They may have arisen, for you, in response to long-term illness. Or a stressful period at work may have left you wondering why you invest so many hours in a job that is highly demotivating. Falling in love, moving to another country, becoming or losing a parent: these are just a few of the experiences that can shift your perspective and cause you to wonder what life might be about. Regardless of circumstances, the big questions are likely to lurk in some corner of our mind throughout our lives, because we are curious and sometimes fragile human beings. These are the questions that shape our soul.

And we have a choice. To push the issues away and fill our lives with noise and activity, allowing a myriad of other pursuits to hijack our attention; or to face them full-on and use them to explore the deepest possibilities of our lives.

So the enquiry 'Does my soul look big in this?', unlike the corresponding query about the size of our butt, is not asked with embarrassment and in fear of a too-honest answer! Instead it expresses eagerness and longing as, in an imaginary changing room, we try on our lives to test out their fit; hoping as we grow older that we may be getting better at handling our relationships and experiences well; trusting that we will be enlivened by the world in which we find ourselves; knowing that to expand our soul is to free ourselves to discover meaning and direction in life; longing to give ourselves the best chance of finding our own voice and of offering our distinctive gifts and insights to others.

If we nurture our souls we will learn more of the equilibrium that equips us to deal with whatever comes our way. The more honest we can be in our response to the questions, the more challenging and creative life will become. We will gradually become less anxious about ourselves, more gracious towards others, more open to unexpected opportunities, more willing to grow. On the other hand, if we do not pay attention to this process, the health of our soul will be jeopardized; it may become parched, bored or constrained, just as our body would suffer if we chose not to feed it.

But what is this 'soul'? It is not some separate and ethereal part of our self that concerns itself only with 'religious' issues. Our soul cannot be pinned down, categorized as physical or spiritual, or excised from the rest of ourselves and examined. It cannot easily be depicted in art, nor, frankly, described particularly well in words. Yet it is important to attempt to describe it, because it is integral to who we are and what this book is about.

What I mean by soul is the sum total of our attitudes, expectations and longings. We are complex beings, forged and influenced by our hormones and our health, our experiences and relationships, what we look like, the weather, our beliefs, dislikes and passions. The soul takes its shape and character from all of this and much more. It emerges from the entire orientation of our lives.

The Hebrew word *nephesh* is sometimes translated soul and also frequently rendered 'life'.[1] The soul is our life force and, not confined to one part of us, has the ability to connect all the different parts. The Franciscan priest Richard Rohr talks about 'the self-defeating game of either–or [an outer life or an inner life], and our need to find the open and gracious space of the limitless, alive, and God-given world that is in-between'.[2] The work of the soul is to interweave our inner and outer selves as well as our inner and outer worlds: so that, for example, we might become wiser about the activities that enliven us and those that deaden our enjoyment; we might understand better the part of ourselves that is touched by particular music; we may realize how a particular relationship is affecting our mental health.

Our soul, our life force, our *nephesh*, which makes us who we are and what we become, is inspired and shaped by countless different things. So this book, as well as drawing on the riches of the Christian faith, embraces many other sources of wisdom that emerge in our lives if we are open to them: the work of novelists, poets, journalists and film-makers; the lives of other people and the issues that are drawn to our attention around the globe; some insights from the Buddhist tradition as well as those of Christian and secular writers.

Of course it also draws heavily on my own life experience with all of its particularities. There will be things held in common with many other people and there will also be some significant differences. I am aware, for example, that when I'm writing I quite often mention my family and children, and I wrestle with how much I should do that. There will be those readers who are long-term or currently single. There will be some who are struggling in difficult marriages. There will be others who have faced or are facing acutely painful issues around fertility. I worry considerably about trampling on people's sensitivities. Yet in the end I can only offer insights from my own life and perspective, and, as my children contribute so much to my learning, their stories are part of what I offer here.

If you're after an $a + b = c$ sort of approach this is not the book for you. Someone once said of my writing that I ask big questions but don't offer big answers, which is true: because for me $a + b = c$ has never been the most fruitful way of exploring life. With others I believe that 'good theology doesn't exactly seek to *give answers . . .*

Rather, good theology is a devising of imaginative strategies *to intensify the enquiry.*[3] The approach you will find here is tangential rather than attempting an equation. It is shaped by the conviction that life lived well and creatively resembles more a labyrinth than a motorway. So if you are looking for clear-cut and definitive answers you will need to look elsewhere. But if you hope to intensify the enquiries of your own soul you may find some use for the stories, metaphors, poetry and quirky connections that fill these pages.

Ultimately *Does My Soul Look Big in This?* is a book that trusts in God as the midwife to all our experiences. The God who draws us into a relationship that is not ethereal, not just in the mind, not simply a pleasant addition to our bodily living and certainly not only concerned with the promise of life elsewhere. Rather, a relationship shaped by the glorious physicality of our daily lives. God's life will spill into your own in unexpected shafts of sunlight and in the moment when a piece of music takes you to a new place within yourself. You will connect with it as you breathe in the scent of wet leaves after rain and you may sense it as you pray for a sick friend to get better. We can only know God in our tangible, created lives.

Through the events and discoveries of our days we learn and relearn the truth that all of life holds the potential to be holy and to speak to us of God's presence, challenge and gratuitous love, which are encountered in the mundane and the extraordinary, the moments of pure joy and the most difficult struggles that we face. In all of this we need to know that if our souls are to grow big enough to encompass the breadth and depth of our potential, they must be awake with expectancy, charged with courage and eternally open to whatever life brings.

1

The John Lewis stages of life
Do things really have to change?

At the marketing agency known as Adam and Eve somebody had a great day when they came up with the John Lewis 'Always a Woman' advertisement. In Spring 2010 it seemed to saturate ITV's commercial breaks and during its first week on YouTube had an astounding 100,000 hits. The ad's 90 seconds consisted of a number of very brief cameos of a woman's life: we watched her from birth through childhood and college, getting married, working, having children and seeing them grow up. Finally she became an elegantly silver-haired grandmother, still very fit and extremely good-looking, striking off across a playing field with her lifelong partner in the company of their bouncing grandchildren and dogs.

The music that accompanied the images was the Fyfe Dangerfield remake of Billy Joel's song 'She's always a woman to me' and its effect was to underline how deservedly loved and appreciated that woman was, knowing where she was going, engaging fully with those around her and relishing life to the full: aided of course by numerous John Lewis products, but that message was cleverly subliminal!

In spite of its trajectory, the advert avoided any sense of a life drawing to its close and was not at all maudlin. Yet every viewing brought a lump to my throat, and if various blogs are to be believed[1] I was not alone. It was incredibly poignant to see somebody's story begin, flourish and mature in a minute and a half. In conveying life's exquisite juxtaposition of beauty and transience, the images hit a rich chord.

The ad also prompted in me some pretty uncomfortable questions: when (or if) I reach the last of the John Lewis stages of life and strike off across that playing field with my partner, our dog and our grandchildren, will I look back and think that at each stage I lived to the full? Will I flick through the photo albums and remember appreciating my carefree childhood, immersing myself in exploratory adolescence, relishing a deeply fulfilled period of parenting, accumulating skills and wisdom in the workplace, enjoying a relaxed engagement with middle age and rejoicing in a gracious silver-surfing retirement? Or will I wish that I had made more of it all, recognized how lucky I was, worked harder at relationships, relaxed more, taken different decisions and focused my time and energy in other ways?

For most of us the different stages of life will offer varying levels of fulfilment and peace. There may have been times when you have felt the flow of life surging through you and ridden the wave, and others when you have been confused, directionless or quite simply unhappy. The John Lewis woman gives the impression of living life seamlessly and without much obvious angst: angst presumably being bad for sales. But outside the world of commercials, in the background of a real life, there would be bemusement and pain as well as the learning and celebrations that characterize what it means to be human.

Rarely, in the living of it, does a real life flow quite so naturally from one stage to another. Each experience requires us to make decisions and negotiate change, with inevitable gains and losses as we go. Take the 'falling in love at university' scenario. It all looks easy for the John Lewis girl, who one moment is blowing out candles on a childhood birthday cake, the next turning to kiss her boyfriend at a student party, the next appearing in a dreamy wedding dress and marrying him.

Our own trajectory in love may have been, or may still be, more precarious than that. As a student there was all that hanging around in the library, hoping in vain that the latest object of your affection would sit down opposite you and ask your name.

Adrenaline-charged moments on station platforms, strategically jumping into the same carriage as she did and keeping your fingers crossed for an adjacent free seat. The randomness and the magic of attraction; the messy, failed relationships. The embarrassingly awkward decisions in love, possibly leading to something good for life, quite possibly not: either way, at some point involving mistakes and heartache.

Not everything falls to happy, golden-hued chance: friendship, jobs, parenting and sexual relationships demand conscious decision-making and a lot of work. In all of this many of us have key moments when we are terribly unsure that we are making the right moves, both on our own behalf and for those dependent on us; and times when we ask ourselves whether we are in the right place doing the right things with the right people.

There may even be periods when you are overcome by a full-blown fear of life moving on. This could be because your confidence has received a severe knock and you doubt your self-worth and your ability to make good decisions. Or perhaps the circumstances of your life have changed beyond your control and not for the better. You might be painfully conscious of the ageing process, of time flying by and all that you might not achieve now: skydiving and Kilimanjaro a fading dream, all-night parties taking far more toll than they used to do! It may be that you feel constrained by the choices you have made in the past, choices that inevitably shape your life today. Should you have been quite so pragmatic in the career path that you have determinedly followed? Are you married to someone with whom you now find it difficult to share your innermost thoughts? For any number of reasons you might fear what is coming next.

Or on the other hand perhaps you are perfectly happy with how things are right now and keen to keep it that way. This could be the best phase of your life so far: why would you want to risk any change? If this is the case then the very hard thing to accept is that nothing, in fact, stays the same for long. Friends move away, the world presents different issues, partners face their own transitions and children grow up. Of course there may be stability in some areas but it is likely that in many ways our lives look different today from how they looked a year ago, or five, or ten.

The Christian Gospels contain one very significant story of transition from the life of Jesus. Jesus comes to the River Jordan to hear the radical and rather notorious new preacher, John the Baptist, and his message of repentance. John is calling upon people to throw out the dross of their lives, to turn themselves around and live differently with a new direction and priorities. Jesus is baptized, marking his commitment to this new way of life, and as part of that experience something about his identity is made clear, to himself and possibly to others. Mark's Gospel tells us that after this happened, 'the Spirit immediately drove [Jesus] out into the wilderness. He was in the wilderness for forty days, tempted by Satan; and he was with the wild beasts; and the angels waited on him'.[2]

The baptism and the wilderness experience represent a significant shift in Jesus' life. Other than the conversation with the devil found in Matthew and Luke's accounts,[3] there is almost no detail about what happened in the desert. Essentially all we are told is that Jesus fasted, was tempted and that angels waited on him. But it is clear that for him the episode triggered the next phase, which he would spend as an itinerant teacher and healer.

I imagine there was a lot of sitting and waiting in those 40 days, praying fervently to survive the harshness of the desert. But because of Jesus' encounter with the devil it also feels like a very dynamic time. Jesus is presented with profound dichotomies and stark choices, tempted by different possible scenarios: feed the world, what a fantastic thing it would be to relieve so much human misery; throw yourself from this pinnacle, prove to yourself and others that there is a God in heaven who cares enough to rescue you; take up your divine right and rule over the nations, you know how well you would do it, and with such consummate good judgement.

Wrestling with these possibilities, Jesus almost certainly sifted the stuff of his life: his thoughts, emotions and experiences to date.

Maybe he clears out the dead wood in order to discern what needs to remain and be built upon: the sort of process we would call de-cluttering. Luke and Matthew tell us that he rejects all three of the 'big ideas' that are so attractive but are just not the right thing at all. He appears to choose a much more difficult way forward and one that is more familiar to the rest of us: a life lived within normal physical constraints, carefully negotiating relationships with other people, looking for signs of the sacred and the holy in the ordinary happenings of life, starting with the mundane and making connections with the extraordinary, probing and exploring his relationship with God rather than being assured of it by some sort of divine mental programming.

The transitions of our own lives too can feel like wilderness moments: disorientating, barren, frightening. But they can sometimes be opportunities to assess what has gone before, to decide what should be taken forward and what needs to be left behind, to discern what can stay the same and what might need to change. Only when we get ourselves in better perspective, only when the empty ambitions and misplaced hopes, the false conceptions of our self and the faux humility have been cleared out, only when we recognize our fragilities as well as our giftedness, will our wilderness be a place where something new can begin to happen, our souls can be enlivened and expanded and we can start to move on.

What is it that God is doing in you at this moment in time that is fresh and creative and that you should nurture? What rubbish do you need to get rid of in order to clear a way forward? What insecurities do you have to acknowledge? What demons do you need to face down? In other words, how will you learn to make confident decisions that will expand your soul? Decisions that will increase your creativity and enjoyment of life, nurture your unfolding self and enable you to take wisdom from one stage of life to the next?

The Buddhist teacher Pema Chödrön has said of religious and spiritual belief systems in general, 'No matter what the teachings are – any instruction of sanity and health from any tradition of wisdom – the point at which they all agree is to let go of holding on to yourself. That's the way of becoming at home in your world.'[4] She suggests that the more we can do this, the greater our capacity to go with the flow of potential in our lives and to deal with change and transition whether it is invited or imposed. Learning to sit a little looser to our picture of ourselves 'manifests as inquisitiveness, as adaptability, as humour, as playfulness . . . We are not trapped in the identity of success or failure, or in any identity at all . . . Every moment is unique, unknown, completely fresh.'[5]

When I first came across these thoughts I was going through a period of fairly intense confusion about myself and my supposed achievements in life. I suddenly understood more fully than I ever had before that I can start again in any given moment of life and do things differently, take a new approach, in some sense set off in another direction.

I read a story in a magazine about a woman who decided to do just that. She left a job in which she was bored in order to spend a year teaching English in Columbia. After the leaving party and the generous present from her colleagues there were two changes in her circumstances: her on–off boyfriend suddenly revealed considerable feelings for her, and a gallery showed interest in the photographic work that until now had just been a hobby. She then made a different decision about which direction to take, recognizing that in fact this was the new life she wanted to pursue.[6]

I don't mean to suggest that by taking a different direction we can cut ourselves entirely loose from our past. What we are today is because of what has happened to us previously. We are shaped by the life stages we have already negotiated and how we have engaged with them. We are what we are because of the things we have chosen to clear out of our lives and the things we have held on to. Our lives carry themes and passions that evolve. A childhood obsession with injustice may have led to a career choice in the law or activism. Friendships formed at school or college might have lasted, the same people being reliable sounding-boards well into maturity. We do not let go of everything as we move on, so there are threads of identity and meaning connecting the baby of the John Lewis advert with the grandmother. But the truth is that we can use that history as a jumping-off point rather than assuming that it constrains us or sets anything in stone. We can choose to do and to be something different in the future.

The idea of needing to let go of some things and take others with us is explored in 'Anatomy of a perfect dive', a poem of incredibly fine balance and poise by the Welsh poet Michael Symmons Roberts. In these short extracts the description of the diver prompts all sorts of questions about the evolution of our own lives.

> *Anatomy of a perfect dive*
>
> Feet on the brink. Avoid brushing earth
> from your soles. Some trace of it
>
> can cross the border with you:
> flecks of other people on your skin and hair,
>
> . . . reach up with your arms, as if this was
> less dive, more surrender,
>
> less surrender, more ascension.
>
> . . . Unlock your knees. Fear is normal.
> Let them hinge and hold. Trust them . . .
>
> Tilt from the top until
>
> your weight, your body, *you*, pulls you
> through the frame like a defenestration.[7]

'Fear is normal,' says the poet. And fear can root us to the spot, or we can unlock our knees in order to make the leap. Finding the courage to go with the transitions of life, to experiment with new challenges, to take opportunities even when we feel unprepared, to let go of our comforting and familiar picture of ourselves and discover what else we can be – all of these things can alert us to capabilities within ourselves of which we have never before dreamed.

The journalist Caitlin Moran writes hilariously of some of the effects of surviving the life-changing experience of childbirth. She says:

> Around the time that a man with giant hands comes towards you with some forceps the size of BBQ tongs, you think, Perspective. Yes, yes I do have some perspective now. I doubt that I will get angry about Norwich Union changing its name to 'Aviva' ever again . . . The high you get as you realise it's all over, and that you didn't actually die, can last the rest of your life. Off their faces with euphoria, and bucked by how brave they were, new mothers finally tell the in-laws to back off, dye their hair red, get driving lessons, go self-employed, learn to use a drill, experiment with Thai condiments, make cheerful jokes about incontinence and stop being scared of the dark.[8]

Childbirth is an experience that some people have: mid-life is one that affects us all. These days mid-life seems to be more of a feeling than a precise age, but at whatever point we think we have reached it, it can be a particularly challenging time to hold on to a coherent sense of our self: a time when we wonder what we are becoming as life leads us rather inexorably, it can feel, through some changes.

Neil LaBute's play *In a Forest Dark and Deep* explores the passions, strengths and vulnerabilities of Betty, a middle-aged woman, who from the outside appears confident and tough. She is a high achiever, a lecturer in English literature who has attained the position of college dean. Until very recently she had a natural confidence in her own considerable sexual allure, but then she fell in love with a student who played her along for what he could gain from her professional position. Falling across the truth in a disparaging email that she was not supposed to read, Betty is devastated and the crisis this precipitates leads to a conversation with her brother in which she describes the experience of growing older and, she believes, losing her attractive edge:

I suddenly saw what it was like to become invisible. You know? To be seen through. I mean, I felt it coming – 'campus' is not for the weak of heart, trust me . . . new, beautiful girls every term, year in and out, and yet . . . I could still turn a head or two. You know, when I tried. Some makeup on and my heels or whatever, yeah. I still had a little something. But it does pass. Yes, it does and one day you are transparent. People walk by and don't see you, you wanna grab them and shake them and yell, 'I am a f***ing beautiful, desirable woman' but you don't . . . because inside somewhere you've begun to recognize the truth. You are not that anymore.[9]

Watching this scene in the theatre I felt, all around me, muted, sharp intakes of breath: women in the audience connecting palpably with what Betty had said.

How we feel about who we are and what we have to offer the world can be disproportionately skewed by a bad hair day. Unless we are pretty unusual, most of us have a degree of vulnerability about how we look. Waking up one day with obviously ageing skin, flabby upper arms and broken, purple veins that used to be in hideable places but are now tracing patterns akin to the Nile delta well below our knee, our sense of confidence and self-worth can quickly erode. A friend commented recently that once you get past the age of 50 it's wise not to have your photograph taken before midday! Looking at my 50-something friends I don't think that's true at all, but I recognize where she was coming from. I admit, sadly, to noticing complete strangers in the street who are probably in their twenties and thinking, 'They have not a clue how beautiful they are.' Beautiful not because they are physically stunning, well groomed or attractive, but just because they are young. They remind me not only that youthful looks are transitory but that I have less time than I used to in which to try new things, be something different and live more.

Yet that is only one way of experiencing middle age. Richard Rohr, who speaks and writes on many issues relating to the human journey, has suggested that our lives are a game of two halves. In the first we are orientated outwards, establishing ourselves and building our relationships, focusing on how we are making an impact and visibly progressing towards goals. In this first half of life we work out our likes and dislikes, our passions and commitments. We construct the container that will hold who we are. This perhaps involves our choice of partner, friends certainly, plus location, job and home.

Then at some point we feel the pull towards a different way of being. All that has gone before prepares us for this, our mistakes probably being more significant than our successes, our awareness of our weaknesses more useful than our knowledge of our strengths. And the key question we find ourselves asking is: what is it for which I have been preparing? What do I really want to do with the rest of my life?

The 'second half of life' is not necessarily about winding down in preparation to stop. It can be immensely energizing as we start to focus on what we really want to do rather than what we feel we ought to accomplish. It is in the midst of this resurgence of energy that we may, happily, notice the truth that in fact it is not youthful skin that guarantees our attractiveness to others. It is the energy that we generate, the vitality that comes from within. It is the liveliness that engages other people and in turn makes them feel alive.

Living with a 'second half of life' attitude, we become much more conscious of wanting every choice about how we spend our time to be an expression of our souls' priorities and longings: what we really believe in, what we really think is important, what we really think we are here for and what truly motivates us and fires that energy day by day. We also get brave about doing new things. In this new phase of life a friend fulfilled a lifetime's ambition to travel across Canada. 'Second phase of life' people might join choirs or sports clubs, learn to fly light aircraft or experiment with sculpture. They start their own business, volunteer or take up meditation.

Conversely, second-halfers become unwilling to fritter away time doing things that feel irrelevant, that do not use their own voice or connect with their passion. Andy Burnham, Labour MP and Shadow Health Secretary, touched on this realization in reflecting on the lost leadership race of 2010:

> Going through the leadership process really changed the way I thought about myself as a politician. Actually, I came to the view that I only really want to do things now that I'm truly passionate about, that are kind of hard-wired inside.[10]

As we move from one stage of life to another we take with us all that we have been, all that we have experienced and achieved, all the previous transitions and crossings over and the brushes with other people that have made us what we are. Each time we face a new situation or relationship, the 'dive' requires us to throw ourselves into the water, a new and different element, in trust. Some of us relish the idea of change, love the 'newness' of what it brings and enjoy the challenge of discovering gifts or enthusiasms that we didn't know we had. Leaving home or starting a new and longed-for job can have this effect. But sometimes change is hard, even brutal, and our overwhelming sense is that of fear, such as when a relationship ends against our will or health issues begin to constrain us. The water closes over our head and we are not sure that we will ever surface. When we do, we may find ourselves changed in ways we had not expected, the task now being to manage the loss and discover the gain.

Whether change is invited and warmly anticipated or imposed and terrifying, in some form or another it is one of life's givens. As the John Lewis stages of our life merge apace from one into another they may look very different, perhaps, from the version in the television commercial: which of course admitted no room for early bereavement, redundancy or ill health; nor simply a different-looking life lived in an urban context or with a same-sex partner.

There are many more versions of life on earth than the John Lewis brand might evoke, but whatever our own life looks like the key to the healthy growth of our soul lies at least partly in the ability to manage the processes of change and being changed, of loss and of gain, of holding on and letting go. Self-acceptance, coupled with the knowledge that we need not stay the same, can be a powerful combination, because the courage to sit loose to ourselves enables us to negotiate transitions wisely, open to the experiences of change that will enlarge our soul. Paradoxically, letting go of our established picture of ourselves can help us to discover who we are. It is to this part of the adventure that we turn next, as we ask how we can become more comfortable in our own skin, gradually finding our distinctive voice and daring to be more fully ourselves.

2

Comfortable in my own skin
Who am I and what do I want to say?

Sometimes I think that my mid-life 'tremor' is fuelled by the strange social situations in which I find myself. There was a party I went to that particularly illustrates this point. It had been a good evening. The crowd was dwindling but there were some hangers-on who showed little sign of needing to go home. Having enjoyed several good conversations throughout the evening with people I like and admire, I felt relaxed enough to stick around and see how things panned out. So there I was in my new dress and confidence-enhancing boots, accepting a last glass of wine from another diehard before collapsing gratefully into an armchair, feeling at ease and comfortable in my own skin.

It was then that it overcame me: a flash of caught-in-the-headlights social clarity as I realized that I was in a minority of one on several measures. I was, self-evidently, the only woman left in the room; I have a northern accent and I am unlikely to be described as urbane; I was probably the only person educated at a state school and a concrete university; I was possibly the only heterosexual, certainly the only parent and therefore the only person who would need to be up for the school run the next day: the rest would be on their knees for Morning Prayer, as this was a gathering of vicars. Even as I clocked how different my life is to that of anyone else in the room, as if to underline my sense of being a creature from another planet the conversation took some intriguing turns: first, to eccentric church organists of the 1980s and then the geography of rural Norfolk. I happen to know nothing about either.

Many of us have experienced the sudden realization that we're having an unexpectedly good time among people very different from ourselves. We have also clung to the edges of the room at parties. When I find myself propping up the wall my knee-jerk response is to wonder what I'm doing here and whether anything I might say will be in the least bit relevant or of interest to others. But I stand firm, shake off my nerves and tell myself that most people manage to muddle on through life without a full-blown identity crisis, even those who face much greater challenges to their self-worth than a gathering of central London clergy. It's just a matter of figuring out what you want to do and say, and how you fit into the bigger picture.

Yet I know from conversations with many friends, acquaintances, colleagues and the huge variety of human beings with whom I have had encounters as a priest, that at some time or another most people struggle with questions about who they are, who they would like to be, what they want out of life and whether they have something distinctive to say and to offer to the world. Many of us find ourselves, perhaps at a particular point in our lives, in a particular context or with a particular set of people, wrong-footed by a nagging dissatisfaction with how we present ourselves and by a sudden sense of unanswered questions churning beneath the surface.

The Turkish writer Elif Shafak, describing her novel *Black Milk*,[1] said:

> We all have different people inside us so in the book there are six different characters: all of them are Elif and all of them are quarrelling constantly, wanting to go in different directions. I realized when I started writing this book that I had no democracy inside me, you know, because I had loved one of those little Elifs – the intellectual, the writer – much more than the others . . . So, throughout the book there is this transformation from a monarchy to a full democracy.[2]

Negotiating between the monarchy and the democracy comes more easily to some than to others. The ecologist and priest John

Rodwell has said, 'I would carve "botanist, priest, husband, father" on my tombstone – perhaps in a circle to avoid people thinking: "Oh, I'm only fourth."'[3] His gently humorous comment recognizes the dilemma of being pulled in a number of directions, being different things to different people. Yet the idea of carving the four words in a circle hints at completeness, the different commitments, passions and relationships of this person coming together to make a coherent whole. It is that whole towards which we need to work if our souls are to be inspired and awakened by the different opportunities of our lives, rather than crushed under the conflict of priorities.

In practice, of course, it is easier to represent this on a tombstone than to achieve it in flesh and blood, where each of us has limitations on our time and energy and difficult decisions to make about how we fit multiple roles into one diary and one life. How do we achieve a creative conversation between the different passions, relationships and projects that shape our lives at each point? How do we live creatively with all of it, without being continually distracted and anxious? Crucially, what is it that defines who we are in the midst of it all?

I once tried to explain to a lifelong friend my dilemmas about what and who I am. She is also 40-something, married and has children of primary school age. Assuming that all middle-aged mothers-of-youngish-children face the same issues I asked in slightly melodramatic tones, 'Who am I after I'm a wife, a parent and a friend?' She looked at me quizzically and asked, 'Why does there have to be anything else?'

Amanda's equanimity is very attractive and reminds me tangentially of the story of Deborah the prophetess. Deborah appears without preamble in the pages of the Hebrew Scriptures, an unexpected feminine presence, the fourth judge in the line-up of Israel's judges and the only woman to have fulfilled that role. Because of her gender she could not appropriately hold court under her own roof, so we are told she sat 'under the palm of Deborah . . . and the Israelites came up to her for judgement'.[4]

In the story that follows she calmly and cleverly engineers the defeat of Sisera, an enemy of her people who has 900 iron chariots at his disposal. We are given no specific insight into Deborah's state of mind but as she summons the warrior Barak, efficiently sets out her battle plan and tells him what he must do, we get the impression of a woman who knows her own mind, accepts the task set before her, and just gets on with it. Barak, presumably knowing a good leader when he sees one, tells her that he'll go to battle if she goes. He feels safe with this unexpected heroine.

When I read Deborah's story the question Amanda posed over coffee that day returns to haunt me, 'Why does there have to be anything else?' I would like more of the equanimity and self-possession, the sense of being comfortable in my own skin, that I see in my friend and in the fourth judge of Israel. Why am I not satisfied with what I achieve and who I am? Why the recurring restlessness?

I suppose one of the obvious answers is that as soon as we have more than one major priority in life there are decisions to be made about which comes first in any given moment, and when those decisions come thick and fast and have no obvious answers, we can feel that we are doing everything badly. My own inability to meld my priorities in a creative way comes to a head in specific, banal but memorable moments – such as the time I prepared a 'Thought for the Day' for BBC Radio 4 while sitting in A&E with our 9-year-old who had injured her knee playing netball. Newspapers spread across the waiting-room table, I hammered away at my laptop, mindful of the imminent deadline, while trying to give Hannah the impression that of course she was my number-one focus and priority at that moment in time!

If our souls are not to be burdened with needless and useless guilt, we have to accept that sometimes there is no ideal solution to an issue and no perfect arrangement to be made; there is no means by which we can carve ourselves up between conflicting demands when there is quite simply an irresolvable clash of priorities. But this is life and we need to give our consciences a break and acknowledge that all we can do is our best, with the tools of intelligence and reflection and the vital ability to rely on other people sometimes. This last skill is not one that I have fully acquired yet, but I'm not alone. At a relatively young age my friend Ros had a double hip replacement operation and was in hospital for 12 days. After she returned home I texted her to ask how she was doing. The reply came, 'I'm back in harness having put a wash on and about to do an Ocado order plus deal with a work thing. Am working out if I can mop the kitchen floor while on crutches.' Handing things over can be tricky, but it's sometimes best for our health.

The stuff about ourselves that we find awkward and unsatisfactory will be different for each of us. We might have a difficult relationship with a family member. Unbeknown to others we may be intensely lonely and longing for a partner or the gift of close friends. We could be struggling in a job that highlights our weaknesses rather than plays to our strengths. Perhaps we are tired of always finding ourselves on the edge of the room at parties, or fighting a permanent sense of exhaustion. Any of this can undermine our sense of confidence and self-worth, diverting a lot of our energy and attention from more fulfilling relationships and activities and leaving us with an unsatisfactory sense of self.

In chapter 3 of his letter to the Philippians, St Paul seems to be wrestling with the same questions. He is filtering what he believes to be really important in his life and choosing to leave behind things that he had previously assumed were definitive, which he now sees as utterly irrelevant. He speaks almost with indignation of the credentials by which he justified himself in the past: a pure-blooded Jew, a Pharisee, a keeper of the Jewish law, vigorous in his attacks on those who deviated from the true faith. Then he concludes, 'I have suffered the loss of all things, and I regard them as rubbish, in order that I may gain Christ.'[5]

The great lesson that Paul has learnt is that he doesn't need this impeccable CV. What he needs is Christ and a relationship with Christ. He no longer reassures himself by a cultural or religious yardstick that he is in, not out. His landscape has shifted entirely and now the process of discovering himself is all about engaging with a person who will remake him from within. 'I want to gain Christ,' he says, 'be found in him, have a righteousness that comes through faith in him. I want to share in his resurrection and his sufferings. Christ has made me his own.'[6] Everything that previously underpinned Paul's sense of self-worth is now seen by him to be irrelevant. It is a huge shift in his internal landscape and it connects with similar experiences that we have as we grow in maturity and recognize that some of the things we had always assumed nurtured our soul do not help us at all.

It also has something to say to us in those times when we feel our centre of gravity going, as we are pulled all ways and struggle to stand up straight. A friend talks of her experience of chronic anxiety, which, when it takes over, threatens to make her life unliveable. What she is learning to do is to recover her equilibrium by focusing on Christ, the expression of God's healing, unconditional and all-encompassing love, the one who is continually reminding us, 'You are who you are, and who you are is more than fine with me.' The one who knows us more intimately than we know ourselves and yet holds and accepts all of it. With St Paul we bring ourselves back time and again to meditate on that radical compassion and to know that whenever we begin to fall because we have forgotten how to stand in our own shoes, then 'underneath are the everlasting arms'.[7]

Our internal tussles about who we are meant to be, what paths we should follow and which relationships would be most life-giving are the fertile ground in which we discover our unique selves. Learning to silence the insidious voice that tells us we are 'not quite good enough' is a key element in the process of growing up. In all of this we are given opportunities to enlarge our souls, to become more open to a range of possibilities that will open doors to what we might become.

We could describe this as a kind of restlessness of the soul, a restlessness that has the potential to tip us down the slippery slope to permanent anxiety, moroseness or even depression. But if we can cultivate a rigorous honesty with ourselves about what exactly we do want out of life, what is really important to us, we can begin to work out how to align ourselves with the things that fuel our passion and make us feel fully alive.

One of the fundamental skills we need in order to be more comfortable in our own skin is the ability to accept ourselves as we are at this moment in time, because our only starting point is here and now and me. In order to engage with the world with a degree of confidence and perspective we need to be sitting comfortably before we begin: before we begin each day, each project, each relationship, each conversation. This self-acceptance has nothing at all to do with complacency. It is not a defensive 'This is me, take me or leave me'. It is much more 'This is me, I understand where it's all come from: now, where shall I go from here?'

Children have far fewer hang-ups than adults about their identity. When our youngest was about two and a half and playing a game of make-believe his sisters would ask him about his character: 'Are you Superman, Joe?' or 'Are you a lion today?' 'NO,' he would shout indignantly, with a fearsome toddler frown, 'I JOE LAIN!' No issue with his sense of self.

For the more mature in years this sort of self-acceptance demands a rigorous and sometimes painful honesty with ourselves. If we are to function as happy and well-adjusted human beings it needs to be our orientation to life, shaping our lifelong journey. True self-acceptance can only come as we learn to know ourselves better: we cannot accept things of which we are not really aware. The more we understand ourselves and our responses to different people, situations and events, the more we can forgive ourselves for our perceived imperfections, let go of the false and distracting concern that we are not all that we should be, rejoice in much of what we are and determine to work on the rest.

The uncomfortable issues about ourselves do not usually go away overnight or get resolved if we ignore them. We can find ourselves having to play the long game with some of them, but we need to be addressing them if our souls are to free us to grow and develop. The alternative approach is to push way down below the surface of our consciousness anything that has the potential to disturb us, hoping that it never rises up again. But even if it doesn't it will continue to influence how we feel, behave and react without us having any handle on the reasons why.

How do people get there, to that place within themselves where they are okay with who they are? By many different routes, I think: the honest and vulnerable conversations that are possible within a close and empathetic friendship; long, solitary walks with the opportunity to think and reflect; adrenaline sports and physical exercise, which purge difficult emotions so that we are more at ease with what is going on inside us; the catharsis that comes through watching theatre, film or television as we make con-nections with characters and situations that resonate for us; experience, which ensures that, for the better, our corners are occasionally knocked off; and, though I hesitate to say this for fear of being quoted out of context, perhaps the judicious use of alcohol, which can enable us in a very healthy way to sit loose to our pride and carefully constructed image of ourselves, and just relax with the person we really are!

Then of course there is therapy. Some of the wisest human beings I know have engaged courageously with the process of therapy (though I hasten to add that many other colleagues and friends who have never sat in the therapist's chair are nevertheless grounded, well adjusted and self-aware). Talking with someone who is skilled at enabling people to explore their own complex-ities can be an extremely effective way of addressing the discomforts and wounds, the perplexity, baggage, pinch-points and triggers that most of us have accumulated by the time we have a decade or two of adult life to our credit.

One of the most debilitating addictions many of us have, and which we need to root out by some means or another, is the sterile habit of comparison: the comparison of our achievements, our relationships and our personalities with those of other people. Most of us struggle with this tendency at some point in our lives and some of us are chronic sufferers. Even if we don't compare ourselves to others we may be painfully aware that others do it for us, which can be equally damaging. Either way it will continually undermine our sense of being at ease with ourselves.

The comparisons do not have to be negative in order, potentially, to distort our self-understanding. I once listened to Chuka Umunna, now Member of Parliament for Streatham in South London, talk about a comparison that others have imposed upon him and how he deals with it. Chuka is of mixed Nigerian, Irish and English descent and is young and good-looking. When he was campaigning door to door he was sometimes asked, 'Are you Britain's Barack Obama?' He replied, presumably with a mixture of political nous and personal wisdom, 'I'd be happy to be Streatham's Chuka Umunna.' And, knowing who he was and where he wanted to be, he got his wish. Being secure in who we are is the starting point for growing, unfolding and discovering all that we have the potential to do and to become.

Writing in the contemporary Christian magazine *Third Way*, the theologian Pete Ward explores the phenomenal interest in celebrity in which many people are caught up. He observes:

> Celebrities offer us possible versions of ourselves. So when we read about them and look at their images we find that we are considering who we might have been, might yet be, or who we would rather be dead than be. Our regard for celebrities has meaning not because of who they are but because of who we are.[8]

So it's not about the celebs, it's all about us. It's partly about exploring who we are through working out who we are not. It sounds almost as though the comparisons could be a useful exercise – except, of course, that our picture of other people's lives is at best partial and at worst completely rose-tinted. We are not comparing like for like when we assess how we are doing in relation to others, whether the comparison is with celebrities or our colleagues and friends. No one can get inside another person's life and see the whole picture: we have to let one another in, as we will see in the next chapter.

The multiple-Oscar-winning film *The King's Speech* explores the inner as well as the outer life of King George VI through the story of his rather bumpy accession to the throne as a result of circumstances wholly beyond his control. His brother Edward's abdication when he famously married Mrs Simpson precipitated George into the limelight. Never having wanted to be King, he finds himself with absolutely no choice, the entire orientation of his life having shifted under his feet overnight. The film explores the young monarch's reluctant struggle, in his new and unbidden role, to find his level, his courage, his identity and quite literally, as he wrestles with a severe stammer, his voice. This part of George VI's story illustrates precisely what we are all doing as we engage with our developing sense of self throughout our lives.

As we learn to be ourselves and only ourselves and discover what a wonderful thing that can be, like St Paul we shed baggage that turns out to have had nothing to do with the essential and hallowed self that we are. The bits of our CV that we had previously thought so significant and impressive, our upbringing, education, qualifications, job title, accent, connections, begin to take a back seat. What matters instead is what we have discovered and come to understand of ourselves, others, the world and God. This demanding and precarious journey will at times involve confusion and fear. But the alternative is to attempt to hold back the tide, to ignore our own potential and the gift of our unique relationships and experiences, and to bury the new and wonderful parts of ourselves that are longing to emerge.

Getting to know and understand ourselves, who we are, what we want to be and therefore want to say, can be so daunting that on occasions we feel muted, unable to find the right words or to get them out of our mouths intelligibly and in the correct order. Yet it can also be an exhilarating and creative experience. The key to relishing our sense of self lies in learning to be comfortable with who we already are and poised to embrace what is emerging. We dig deep, knowing that we have particular gifts to offer, perspectives that no one else commands, and a distinctive voice to find. Comfortable in our own skin, knowing who and what we are, bringing the particular insights of our soul to our encounters with the world and one another, we are reassured by the presence and encouragement of the one who gently and firmly calls us to become all that we – and only we – possibly can be.

3

The school playground
Will I ever be 'in' with the 'in crowd'?

For most of my life I have struggled to find my feet in school playgrounds. When I was seven my Dad got a new job and we moved from the village where we had lived for the first seven years of my life to a town some distance away. The news quickly spread around the unfamiliar schoolyard that I was the 'new vicar's daughter'. It would have felt better just to be Rosemary, no strings or expectations attached, but the introductions were beyond a 7-year-old's control.

Years later, moving to secondary school, I wasn't surprised to discover that the playground was the natural territory of those who were more popular, more confident or frankly cooler and tougher than I was. And because my dad knew some of the staff at my new school, again the 'vicar's kid' label preceded me. I vividly remember the religious studies teacher booming down the corridor, 'I wouldn't expect to see *you* running in school, Rosemary Priestley.'

These experiences awakened in me a sense of being on the edge of the crowd, a feeling that has never been entirely put to rest. Even now, as a mother at the school gate, I assume that everyone else knows everyone else and is nearer the centre of the action than I am. I have a residual sense that people probably think I'm a bit weird. And I invariably suppose that the 'in crowd' is over in the far corner, coded and impenetrable.

So it was a moment of revelation when at a party a friend introduced me by saying, 'This is Rosemary: I stand with her in the playground because she knows everyone and then they talk to me too.' I couldn't have felt less like that person she described but I suppose I should have guessed that a lot of people feel the same way as I do, on the edges and a little on edge, assuming that everyone else is perfectly at home. Fear, nerves, shyness, defensiveness, a sense of feeling small and struggling to find our place: playgrounds bring these things out in many of us, and grown women and men can find themselves feeling, and sometimes acting, like 7-year-olds.

Of course the schoolyard is by no means the only context in which people struggle to find their place. The MP Andy Burnham talks about his experience of coming from what he describes as an ordinary working-class background and ending up at Cambridge and in Parliament. He comments:

> In the leadership contest, I said: 'I've always expected a tap on the shoulder – you know, 'Come on, mate, you're not meant to be here' – and it really connected with people . . . a lot of people told me 'I really understand that, and I really feel that that's me as well'.[1]

Our sense of belonging with other people, sometimes so strong, can at other times be very precarious.

Some of us live with this shaky sense of belonging throughout our lives, whether because of an early life experience or simply as a result of circumstance or personality. It can sometimes be very isolating and undermining. But being on the edge of a crowd, an institution, a friendship group or even a family can also be a good thing. The edges can hold resources which feed our understanding of life and change our expectations. There are advantages to the perspective that is offered by a little distance: a clarity and an objectivity that we can access more easily from a position a little way away from the action. Being outside the 'in crowd' can have as many upsides as being the most popular child on the street.

Borderlands and edges are boundaries where we can access two worlds and two sets of experiences. They offer us the chance to reflect and to experiment. On the edges you can have one foot in what is known, accepted and understood and another placed, in the first step of exploration, out in the unknown. If you are on the edges at work you can engage with the insights of your colleagues while looking at new possibilities. You can reassure people that you are standing with them on familiar ground, yet begin to enthuse them about other possible ways of doing things. If you are on the edges of more than one friendship group you can make introductions that result in new relationships. If you are married to someone who works in a different professional world than your own you can take the lessons of one context and apply them in another.

On the edges we often find artists, musicians, poets and writers, those who are a conduit for innovative thoughts and ideas. Which is perhaps why Jesus was always hanging around the margins and crossing boundaries. He traversed lakes and the waters of the Jordan. He crossed into the land of the Samaritans and into their lives, even the lives of their women. He contravened people's patience, their social sensibilities and their expectations. And he was an itinerant of no fixed abode, part of an alternative community who were on the edges of society.

It is possible to find yourself, for all sorts of reasons, both on the margins and in the centre and therefore playing a very specific role. In many senses this was true of Jesus too. It was also true of Esther, who was both at the centre of the establishment and part of a marginalized constituency, and whose story is told in the book that takes her name.

Esther was an orphaned Jewish woman living in Persia who was brought up by her cousin, Mordecai. When King Ahasuerus recruited a new wave of women to his harem, Esther, who was very beautiful, was included, but Mordecai warned her to keep her Jewish identity secret. Winning the King's admiration, Esther is crowned as Queen, but events almost implode when the King's most senior official turns against the Jewish people in their entirety because Mordecai refuses to pay homage to him, and persuades Ahasuerus to allow him to kill all of the Jews in the kingdom.

Mordecai appeals to Esther's sense of self, identity and destiny by saying to her:

'If you keep silence at such a time as this, relief and deliverance
will rise for the Jews from another quarter, but you and your father's
family will perish. Who knows? Perhaps you have come to royal
dignity for just such a time as this.'[2]

Esther asks for a fast to be held on her behalf, confirms that she
will do it and takes her life in her hands when, against all the rules,
she enters the King's presence urgently without being summoned.
In doing so, she saves the life of her people. Whether we are on the
margins of the crowd, at the centre or in some sense occupy both
positions, our actions have an impact on others. This interaction,
one with another, encourages and enlarges our soul.

In 2009 and 2010 T-mobile ran a series of adverts with the
strapline 'Life's for Sharing'. Filmed in Liverpool Street Station,
Trafalgar Square and an arrivals hall in Heathrow Airport, the
ads brought together performers and unsuspecting members
of the public in mass sing-alongs and dance routines. On each
occasion a crowd of disparate human beings, previously complete strangers to each other, morphed into a community, sharing
smiles, tears and exclamations of delight. Elderly women waved
their walking sticks to Kool and the Gang, Trafalgar Square rang
out with 13,000 voices singing 'Hey Jude', and at Heathrow a
pair of recently reunited lovers were serenaded by complete
strangers.

Being an optimist about human nature and longing to believe
that there lurks in all of us, just below the surface, the desire to
be part of one big happy family, those adverts used to make me
smile. But they also touched that part of me that sometimes feels
a little too much on the margins of the playground, and I used
to wonder what effect they might have on someone who was
chronically lonely. The message that it's easy to connect and great
fun to be part of a crowd is harsh and unpalatable for someone
who is feeling isolated. Or even for those whose tricky experiences in their early years have left a mark in adulthood.

Finding our place in the world inevitably involves negotiating
relationships with other human beings. For many of us, though

not all, the search for a life partner has an impact for at least part of our life on much of our major decision-making: the jobs we take, how we choose to spend our free time, where we choose to live. Longing to find someone with whom we can share everything is a powerful driver for the way that we live our lives. It can be an issue that pervades our subconscious mind even when we are not actively thinking about it. We hope at some stage to meet someone who will, for ever, share our deepest longings and fears, our plans and dilemmas, our passions and celebrations. The disappointment when a new relationship does not develop as we had hoped, or a more established one hits a wall, can be deeply disappointing and very painful.

It can be dangerous to romanticize romance. Sexual relation-ships that work are as much a product of the willingness to listen, learn, negotiate and empathize as they are the result of a chance happy collision or the meeting of eyes across a crowded room. You can bet that most people who stay together for several decades have put in some sheer hard graft along the way! The harsh reality is that some people put in the graft only to find their relationship crumbling, sometimes sooner, sometimes later.

Others who are more than ready to listen and negotiate, to commit themselves to the give and take of life lived with the privilege and challenge of sexual partnership, just do not seem to be in the right place at the right time to meet someone with whom they might do that for very long. I hope it doesn't sound too 'Sex and the City' to say that experimenting with potential partners, although wonderful at times, is for most people some of the time and some people a lot of the time a tentative and precarious process. Ultimately the whole enterprise of looking for someone with whom to share our life and home is risky.

Similarly, learning to belong among colleagues or cultivating a friendship are skills that we acquire through sometimes getting it right and sometimes getting it wrong. I fell accidentally into a new friendship by making a chance remark to the stranger standing next to me as we watched our children's swimming lesson. It has evolved into a warm and easy rapport. Equally I have sometimes cursed my natural tendency to connect without making at least a cursory assessment as to whether I might regret it: getting out of a friendship can be harder than getting in! We learn by our successes but also by our mistakes, sometimes being hurt and sometimes hurting others. And all of this has an impact on our soul, because our past experiences can ensure that we are open to new relationships or cause us to be closed. They can lead us to be expectant of good things from other people, or suspicious of how they might damage us.

Perhaps it is not surprising that we are sometimes tempted to avoid the irritations and vicissitudes of other people and to opt for an easier life. On a long journey south, coming home from a visit to my mother, there were no seats available when I boarded the train at Preston. As we pulled out of the station the train manager reassured us over the intercom: 'I do apologize for the current overcrowding but historically we tend to lose a lot of people at Wigan and Warrington, so hopefully you will be able to find a seat after that.'

What a delightful way of dealing with an overcrowded life: just shed a few people whom you can do without! You might be tempted by this option because you have been put off human relating by some key relationships in the past that have undermined your happiness or your confidence. Or you might simply have found some people too hard to understand, relate to or learn to love. One way of responding is to shut yourself off to the possibility of having to connect with anyone who doesn't look or sound similar to you. Yet this may well be a way to avoid your own issues and vulnerabilities, to close yourself off not only to others but to what they might teach you of yourself. You may feel safer but you will probably also recognize, deep within yourself, that you are missing the opportunity to grow. That your soul is closing down rather than opening up.

Our daughter Olivia came home from school one day and told us proudly that her name had been placed in the 'Golden Book', a privilege reserved for those who have achieved something special. Olivia told us 'It was for including everyone in the playground in my games – *even when I didn't want to*.' I didn't like to enquire quite how the teachers knew that she'd included 'those she didn't want to' and how those particular children felt about this slightly dubious hospitality, but I did find myself hoping that Olivia will be secure enough in herself to carry this habit into later life. If we can be sufficiently comfortable in our own skin to welcome into our space those with whom we have no natural affinity we may find unexpected connections and revelations.

Most people have a reasonably strong impulse to connect with others, though we seem to be on a wide spectrum from 'very self-contained' to 'highly gregarious'. We also prefer different ways of relating. Some find that there is no substitute for meeting up face to face, for being physically present to one another in 'real time'. Others love the tangential connections that develop as part of exploring relationships and networks on the internet and seem never happier than when they are sitting alone somewhere, connecting with hundreds of Facebook friends. We should also remember that it is possible to be entirely alone yet fully engaged with the wider human community as we read a novel or newspaper or listen to the radio and pick up new ideas and inspiration from others.

Email exchanges can be like a speeded-up version of snail mail, and may provide the same opportunity to share the thoughts, questions, personal information and soul-searching on which friendships are built, though perhaps more quickly and in a more intense way. Many of us have a 'mixed economy' of friendships, some as the result of making time to meet up, month by month, year on year, in person, others that develop primarily through cyberspace, and many that embrace both realities.

In an article about Mumsnet, the popular internet site where parenting issues are hotly debated and childcare dilemmas shared, Kerry Kidd tells a lovely story of a cyber connection leading to a neighbourly encounter in real life:

> I'm recovering at home after an operation. A friend turns up at the
> door. She brings the children comics and buys them sweets, does
> some housework and has a friendly cuppa. The usual response of
> a good friend, or a fellow churchgoer. The difference is, we share
> no faith and I have never met her before. Our connection is through
> Mumsnet, the website with a million monthly users.[3]

The key to the value of such forms of relationship is surely that
if we are not to be left adrift in a half-life in cyberspace, what we
are 'out there' needs to relate in some real way to what we are in
the rest of our life. The question is: how genuinely in relationship
are we with those people? This is the litmus paper, the acid test. Of
course it applies to face-to-face relationships as well, but if it is
an internet relationship the issue is perhaps more complicated.

Ultimately, through whatever media we choose to pursue
our relationships with others, it seems that only a very small
minority of people exist happily in relative isolation and few
would choose to come to the end of their lives alone. My father
was a parish priest for 30 years. He said that some of the saddest
funerals at which he officiated were those at which the only people
who joined him were the funeral director and a representative
from the residential care home where the person had died.

Of course we will differ, depending on how extravert or introvert we are, in the extent to which we are enlivened by the company of other people or by time spent alone. But in one sense we
are incomplete without others. There is much that we cannot
experience first-hand because our life is so necessarily particular.
It helps to know other people's truths in order to interpret our
own.

In an interview in the *Church Times* the priest and ecologist
John Rodwell muses:

> I have unmet longings – to be more fully known as the person
> I really am: ambiguous, stubborn, needy. Augustine is centrally
> concerned with this restless, unsatisfied sense. There's an inter-
> weaving of longings. What I want to ask him is, has it been met,
> mate?[4]

This connection between knowing and being known, loving and being loved, understanding ourselves because we are understood, is at the heart of our need to relate to others. St Paul writes of this longing in his first letter to the Corinthians, eloquently describing the process of growing up, spiritually and mentally. 'When I was a child, I spoke like a child, I thought like a child, I reasoned like a child; when I became an adult, I put an end to childish ways. For now we see in a mirror, dimly, but then we will see face to face. Now I know only in part; then I will know fully, even as I have been fully known'.[5]

I suspect that one of the most painful and debilitating aspects of losing a lifelong partner is the knowledge that the person who knew us best and most fully is now irrevocably absent from the world in which we must continue to live out our lives. How will we ever be fully known again? How could anyone begin at the beginning and build up that knowledge and understanding? Yet the flipside of this is the positive legacy of being known and accepted for what we are over several decades. What a huge contribution that makes to a person's sense of self-worth. Being with others gives us a fuller picture of ourselves, providing us with contrasts, reference points and shared reactions. We variously inspire, provoke, energize, move, complete or challenge one another. These are some of the ways in which we grow. And through one another we acquire a sense of belonging in the world and in our communities. Whether we find ourselves mostly at the margins of communities, generally in the heat of the action, somewhere between the two or in different places at different times, the people we live among are our greatest challenge and our greatest gift, as together we learn to see and know ourselves and others better.

Sometimes the key to belonging in the playground isn't just about putting insecurities aside, nor just learning those difficult lessons about negotiation, sharing and taking turns. It's about recognizing that everyone belongs and behaving in a way that reflects that understanding. The reality being that there will always be those with whom we find it harder to play, but they might yet be the ones who can challenge us to understand new things about ourselves.

It doesn't matter whether we are 'in' with the 'in crowd'. What does matter is how our own particular arrangement and depth of relationships is growing and developing. Smiles in the street and the kindness of strangers can do more to make us feel part of the human community than the feeling that we are in the biggest and loudest gang in the playground. It's something about being seen and acknowledged, and it gives us confidence and peace with ourselves.

Anne Michaels' novel, *Fugitive Pieces*, is the story of Jakob, a young Jewish refugee who is rescued from a massacre in Poland by a Greek man called Athos. On his precarious journey to safety, while hidden in the back seat of the car or huddled against Athos under a blanket, Jakob is mourning the loss of his parents and his sister Bella, whom he knows to have been brutally killed in the conflict he has fled. Jakob tells us, 'Bella clung. We were Russian dolls. I inside Athos, Bella inside me.' And as he shares his misery with the utter stranger who has risked everything to be his lifeline, Athos tells him, 'We must carry each other. If we don't have this, what are we?'[6]

The next chapter will explore the idea that nurturing our soul is a process inextricably bound up with geography, journeying, place and home. It is also profoundly about the people we are with. Being on the edges of the playground can hold as much potential as being right at the heart of the action. Having one foot in the borderlands and the other in the centre can be exciting, if a little stretching at times. Finding ourselves reflected in one another and also differentiated, holding each other in times when that is all that we can do – these are some of the key ways in which we grow our soul. Sometimes as friends, partners or family, what we can do best is hold and contain one another as in turn we are simply held. 'Bella clung. We were Russian dolls. I inside Athos, Bella inside me.'

4

Born in the North
Where on earth is home?

———◆◆———

When I was a teenager I wore a T-shirt that declared in bold white lettering on a black background, 'Born in the North, Exist in the North, Die in the North: Lancashire'. Migrating south to Canterbury in the late 1980s I took that T-shirt with me. It might have played unhelpfully into the stereotype of the northerner with narrow horizons, but for three years I wore it in the flatlands of Kent with a sense of irony. Born and brought up in East Lancashire, I have always had a strong sense of my northern roots. Defensive about the disparaging stereotypes of northerners and the North – grimy industrial landscapes, chips with everything, ferrets, flat caps and Hilda Ogden lookalikes – I celebrated unashamedly the blunt honesty, dry humour, gentle mists and green hills that nurtured my childhood and adolescence.

Our souls are undoubtedly shaped by the landscape and the culture of our upbringing and I continued to wear my 'Die in the North' T-shirt long after deciding to live in the South. But the influence of our physical surroundings and the social heritage we carry does not stop when childhood ends. Throughout our lives, wherever we go, we are shaped by the sounds and the colours, the climate, the sights and scents that surround us. Whether we travel a lot and frequently relocate our home or spend most of our life in the same place, we become what we become at least partly because of the places in which we have belonged over the years.

I vividly remember getting off a train in St Andrews, Scotland, for the first time. I was awed by the wild beauty of the beach, the breakers and the sheer expanse of sea and sand. I found myself wondering what influence that distinctive physical landscape has on the lives and aspirations, the spiritual thoughts and understanding of those who call it home. What does it do to their souls? Do they live with a sense of vast possibilities, endless adventures and the desire to ride the crest of the wave? Or do they struggle with emptiness and surges of existential terror? Are they particularly sensitized to the idea that in the vast beyond of the swelling waves is the inexorable creativity that is God? Or does the periodic violence of the waters evoke fear and the suspicion of a hostile creator?

Perhaps the answer is 'none of the above'. It may be that to the residents of St Andrews the waves are simply waves and the expanse of the sea is just that. But I suspect that for many of us our physical environment really does have an impact on our soul. Having spent my entire childhood and adolescence among green hills, I find flat landscapes a bit depressing. They give me a sense of life setting out, all at once, its entire stall: nothing hidden; no surprises over the next rise because there is no rise; no mystery. Yet I imagine that some people find valleys and hills claustrophobic if they have grown up where there is always a huge sky and the horizon is distant. Perhaps level and open ground speaks to them of space, potential and possibility.

The sheer physicality of a location can have an effect on our soul. I have struggled with this truth since becoming a parent, because people frequently assume that cities are not a good environment in which to bring up young children: the expectation is that if you start a family you will move out. Three children down the line we are still here. There are very big parks a short walk away and we are lucky enough to have access to beautiful communal gardens. The decision to stay is conscious and deliberate and as much to do with the advantages of the city for our children as for us.

Our eldest daughter was four years old when we moved from a flat just off Trafalgar Square to a more residential part of London. Walking the streets around our new home she struggled one day to explain to me why her new surroundings made her feel different. It transpired that she missed the buzz, the bustle and the soaring buildings that had shaped the first few years of her life. At nine years old, Hannah retains a strong sense of nostalgia when we return to the Strand and Trafalgar Square. She still misses the spaces that formed her earliest neural connections. They quicken her soul in a way that the quieter parts of the city do not.

Yet in recent years I have read magazine articles that tell me about the greater advantage of 'green exercise' and others that argue for the psychological benefits of waking up to a view of fields and hedgerows rather than an industrial landscape. So I have asked myself: is there an inbuilt negativity about the city landscape itself, something that suppresses the spirit, which is unavoidable and which it is irresponsible for us to inflict on our children?

The matter was unexpectedly settled for me when, one beautiful autumn day, we visited friends who have moved to Wiltshire. They have what can only be described as an idyllic new home: a house you could easily get lost in, with several acres of back garden stretching down to the waters of the River Avon. Our three children, set free like puppies in this beautiful green space, rolled blissfully on the grass, foraged for fallen apples and swung on the tree swing that I swear came straight out of Anne of Green Gables. As our youngest pointed to a field just across the river and asked, 'Is that a sheep or a cow?', I remembered my childhood incredulity when told that some urban children grow up not knowing where milk comes from!

Just as I was making a mental note to do an internet property search at the earliest opportunity, our friends' four grown-up children strolled out into their parents' new garden. They were brought up in a flat on Trafalgar Square, next door to the one in which we lived during Hannah's early childhood. Each of them is grounded, lovely, free-spirited and comfortable in their own skin, equally at home in that garden and the various towns and cities in which they have now settled. From that moment I stopped worrying that the city will constrain our children's souls. (I have yet to deal with the pollution.)

Of course, as well as the physical landscape, it is the events and experiences that we associate with particular places that have a powerful effect on who and what we become. For many of us the places in which we grew up have marked and shaped us most powerfully, either because our experiences there were good and nurturing or, on the contrary, damaging and painful. For the majority, perhaps, the truth will lie somewhere in between.

The magazine *Psychologies* runs a regular strand which is effectively a psychotherapy session involving an anonymous participant. One of these sessions was with a woman who had returned to live in the town where she grew up after a number of years away. A host of issues immediately began to prey on her mind concerning an incident that had occurred there in her late teens. Her father had wanted her to work in his shop rather than go to college, so she chose to pursue her college course while sometimes working for him. One day she told her dad that she had to revise and couldn't work, so he asked her younger brother and sister to cover for her. While she was away someone came into the shop and robbed them at gunpoint. Her father always blamed her for not being there and her relationships with her family had never been the same after that.

The impact of that history had never gone away altogether while the woman lived elsewhere, but she had managed to hold the pain at arms' length. Back 'home', that was no longer possible and her life became unmanageable to the point that she could barely cope with leaving the house. It took a very honest addressing of the events of the past to free her from the impact of the bad associations.[1]

It matters where we came from and what it did to us, offered us, took or withheld from us; how it nurtured or scarred us, gave us a second and third chance or none. It may have done a number of those things, good and bad. Undoubtedly it will have been a significant influence on what we are, whether because it nourished our soul well and gave us the confidence to live fully and with trust in others, or starved us of affection and made us wary, suspicious or over-dependent on their approval. Making peace with the place where we are from can be at least part of the process of integrating our past and present.

In her quirky and poignant memoir *Your Voice in My Head*, Emma Forrest explores the idea that a place can, by its physical characteristics, nurture our mind and our spirit. Recovering at a rehabilitation centre after a suicide attempt she reflects:

> The grounds are very beautiful at the Priory . . . One expects to see peacocks, and I imagine there must be patients who, in fact, do see peacocks. It is a place for a gothic love affair. It isn't until I leave that place that I go out and find love for the first time. That could be because I got well (I doubt it) or because the grounds have, by osmosis, worked their way into me. This is love: beautiful, secret, overgrown, last chance.[2]

We often recognize instinctively the places in which our souls will be liberated to thrive most fully. We know the sorts of environment that bring out the best in us. There are holiday places we will remember for ever because of the way that they nurtured our body and mind, whether because we learned something new, ate wonderful food, feasted our eyes on a sight that inspired us, slept under the luminous majesty of the stars, felt the electricity of South American salsa, experienced the African earth as a homecoming, met people who made us think differently, or simply felt nurtured by the warmth of the Mediterranean sun. There are layers of experience in us all that have accumulated in a myriad of different places. Some of those places in particular have energized our soul and drawn out more fully the person that we were created to be.

In the Hebrew Scriptures we sometimes find people naming places in honour of the experiences they have had there. Two stories from the life of Jacob illustrate this custom beautifully.

There is the incident that takes place when he is fleeing from his brother Esau, who is quite rightly livid with him for stealing his birthright. Jacob stops to sleep and dreams of a ladder raised to heaven, with angels ascending and descending continually. God promises Jacob the land on which he lies and numerous offspring 'like the dust of the earth', who will spread to the east, west, north and south.

When he wakes up and recalls the encounter with God, Jacob cries, 'How awesome is this place! This is none other than the house of God, and this is the gate of heaven.'[3] He sets a stone there as a pillar and pours oil over it, as though it is an altar on which to give thanks. And he calls the place Bethel, meaning 'House of God'.[4] There he has had an encounter which has changed his understanding and picture of his own future, energized his soul and re-aligned his relationship with God.

Later in Jacob's story there is another striking interlude when he is on the way, as instructed by the Lord, to visit the aggrieved brother from whom he has wisely been keeping a safe distance. Sending his cattle and household ahead of him, Jacob is left alone and finds himself wrestling with a man traditionally interpreted to be an angel. They struggle until dawn and the man-angel wounds Jacob, blesses him, and gives him the new name of Israel. His own name is changed as an affirmation of what has happened to him, then Jacob (Israel) renames the place in which this has happened. He calls it Peniel, which means 'face of God', explaining, 'For I have seen God face to face, and yet my life is preserved.'[5]

When we have experiences that change the direction of our lives, charge our souls or save us from an approaching danger perhaps we should find ways of 'naming' and 'marking' the place in which they happened. If not literally, we can do this by putting a mental marker in the sand, in our imaginations soaking the ground with oil. Or we might keep a handful of soil, a pebble from a beach, an image that evokes the landscape, a photograph of the building in which we encountered God: anything that continues to connect us with the place in which we were changed.

What will we name the places that hold a deep significance for us? How will we mark out the ground? What gesture is our equivalent of Jacob pouring oil over the rock? Remembering and somehow anointing the significant places in our lives can help to embed the experiences we have had there, the changes that were wrought, the understandings that were elicited and the affirmations with which we were blessed. Places can resonate profoundly with our soul.

If places shape us and different places shape us differently, it is no surprise that pilgrimage, the act of journeying with the conscious intention of growing our souls, is a very ancient and deeply rooted urge. People have always journeyed and their journeys have sometimes been for the specific purposes of worshipping or asking God's advice. Our modern journeys can connect us with these previous sojourners, and the sense of human beings journeying and searching, wandering, wondering, longing and questioning can be very powerful as we explore some of the same big questions that have characterized people's experiences of pilgrimage for thousands of years.

John Pritchard touches on the power of pilgrimage and journeys when he describes a day spent walking in the Sinai desert, where Moses is said to have received the Ten Commandments.

> We determined to spend the first two hours of the day walking in complete silence, drinking in the profound otherness of the desert. It was magical. We walked in the shadow of the people of Israel, searching for their new home. We walked in the shadow of the desert fathers, going out into the wilderness to face their demons. We walked in the shadow of Jesus, taking to the desert to have it out with the devil. We walked in our own shadow, examining our life journeys, our motivations, our vulnerabilities.[6]

Pilgrims across the ages are united by the experience of travelling as an impetus to search their own souls. But sometimes those journeys have been enforced rather than chosen. Yahweh's followers were an archetypal displaced community, living among the

Egyptians and later the Babylonians, spending generations wandering in the desert of Sinai, much of the time with very little hope of ever putting down roots. In the Hebrew Scriptures and in twenty-first-century life there are many stories of people who are 'dis-placed' and we learn much from them about the impact of an enforced journey or an unbidden exile on the growth of the soul. They may be people who have lost their land and property through war or natural disaster; they might have been ejected from their home; they could have chosen to flee for their own safety; they may have run as fugitives, thrown themselves on the mercy of another country, spent time in temporary accommodation. If they are among the more fortunate of refugees or migrants they have found somewhere to make a new home, but the loss, the disorientation and the journey itself will undoubtedly have changed them.

I remember, as a solicitor's clerk assisting with asylum applications, interviewing Bosnian refugees about their journey to the United Kingdom. Their security and sense of belonging in a place had been brutally removed and here they were, building life from scratch in a place where they neither understood the culture nor spoke the language. Some had formed relationships on their journey as, crammed together in the back of lorries, they looked after one another and frequently faced grave danger.

For some people the journey becomes very much the thing that makes them who they are. They form relationships along the way and discover what really matters to them as they go. It is likely that Abram was a nomad even before God told him, 'Go from your country and your kindred and your father's house to the land that I will show you.'[7] But he was being called to travel further, discover more, and together with his wife Sarah become part of the story of God's abundance in populating the world. God promised to be with him, to give him numerous descendants and to bring them to a new home. Whether or not this seemed likely to Abraham and Sarah, they went. It was the beginning of a relationship with the God who would accompany them all the way. And it was as they travelled that they discovered themselves and their purpose.

At some point people who have been displaced, chosen to make a journey or lived as refugees may successfully put down new roots but they will always be shaped by the places from which they have come as well as those in which they settle. They will almost certainly have been changed by whatever they experienced on the way. They may at some point have stopped seeing themselves as migrants and found the strength to know that they can settle pretty much anywhere and make a new life, because under the most terrible of pressures they have found within themselves the resources to survive.

Adam Weymouth writes, 'A migrant is one who is displaced from his home; he is defined by definition of where he is not. The nomad differs from the migrant in that he has no fixed home, and instead he is at home everywhere', and goes on to suggest that 'During the course of the journey, the pilgrim moves from seeing himself as a migrant, to seeing himself as a nomad, at home in the world. He who walks the way until he becomes one with it. He is not only at home in the world, he is the world. The world is at home in him.'[8]

This reminds me of my friend Sarah, who spends different parts of the year living in different places. She says that she doesn't know where she'll eventually settle because there are so many locations in which she can imagine being happy and making a home. Sarah does give me cause to wonder about my own inability to live outside Zone One of the London Underground, and whether that might be due to some deep-seated issue that I ought to resolve! There are people who are truly at home wherever they go, possibly because they are unafraid of change and transition, comfortable in their own skin and able to find their place among others as well as being at ease on the edges of the crowd. This gives a sort of inner confidence that enables them to be at home in the world wherever they are, and the world to be at home in them. It also points us towards a clearer definition of home: it is a condition within ourselves of being poised, comfortable and at ease. A condition that can be nurtured or undermined by our surroundings, but in the end a state of heart and mind, a state of soul, rather than a location outside of ourselves. Home is a place within ourselves that recognizes the presence of God everywhere.

In his deeply insightful and often hilarious book, *Strangely Warmed: Reflections on God, Life and Bric-a-Brac*, Andrew Rumsey, Vicar of Gipsy Hill in South London, writes about a Good Friday walk with the congregation of his church. At various places along the way hymns are sung and the parish is prayed for by those who live and worship there. Describing the scene when the group stops at a particular junction near a Tube station, Rumsey's words are redolent with the idea that place is hugely significant, because every place is potentially sacred:

> It . . . is a peculiar mix of white and black, posh and poor, and we meet with our song-sheets flapping where the junkies score and professionals pour out up the hill. Here might we stay and sing, inviting ridicule. For no holier place exists, and nobody there would be anywhere else.[9]

Our relationship with a place is partly about its geography, partly about its history and how it has become intertwined with our own, partly about our current associations with it. That relationship is fed by the ways in which we cherish, remember and value a place, the significance which we afford to it, how we name and mark a location in our minds to make sure that we know what happened to us there and do not forget it. In all of this we may come to realize that every place has the potential to nourish our well-being and our growth. It does not need to have been marked out by others as 'spiritually significant' in order to be holy for us.

There is nowhere that God is not and therefore nowhere that is not sacred: if we really believe this we will recognize the holy in every form of life on every street corner. Gradually we will learn to feel at ease with ourselves wherever we happen to be or to go.

Our soul's restlessness can become a positive energy, leading us to new places and new discoveries, while at the same time we are rooted and grounded wherever we are, at home in ourselves, sensing how we have been shaped by the places we have known. As we grow in our understanding of how we have been affected and energized by the places we have explored, journeyed through, engaged with and called home, we are poised for the challenge of connecting that experience with the complexities of the wider world.

5

This gossamer web
Can we make sense of the world?

If you have ever wondered at the pattern of a pine cone, the spiral of a seashell, the intricacy of an unfolding fern or the arrangement of seeds in the golden head of a sunflower, you have witnessed the occurrence in nature of the Fibonacci sequence. In the world of maths this is a series of numbers where each is the sum of the previous two. But as well as having various mathematical applications its imprint is found in architecture, art, music and the natural world, arguably even occurring in the breeding proclivities of rabbits!

Just as the places of our childhood, the landscapes through which we travel and the homes that we make for ourselves as adults, leave an imprint on our souls, so too our experience of creation and our global community forms and shapes our sense of self, nurturing the life force, the *nephesh*, within us. The question of whether or not any of it seems to add up or to connect in any way, whether there are any correlations, links or patterns, is one of the big questions of life. At times, when none of it appears to make sense, we can feel out of control, adrift in an alien world, struggling to find direction in our own life or a point to any of it. At work a project in which we had invested a lot of time and meaning suddenly fails. In our close social network a friend is taken ill with something life-threatening. Or at home, completely out of the blue, our partner leaves us. In these sorts of circumstances it can be hard to believe that life makes sense or that we can rely on the world to be kind.

Yet there are moments in our lives when the world seems full of patterns, correlations, connections and recurring themes. What happens in one place seems to relate, unexpectedly, to events in another. A friend shares some thoughts which are voiced by some-one else in an entirely different context a few days later. We read a randomly chosen novel and it happens to resonate with an issue currently in the news. We learn something new and then stumble across several references to the same subject within a short space of time.

When these things happen it is relatively easy to believe that if we pull at this thread or that in our human experience we will dis-cover things that connect. We begin to hope that life in the world is a web that we can navigate with some degree of confidence, at least partly prepared for what we might come across next because it is likely to contain some sense of relatedness and familiarity.

Yet we have a parallel experience of the world that undermines all of this. Most of us have moments, some of us many of them, when we suspect that contrary to our hopes nothing actually adds up or has anything to do with anything else. Events seem random and meaningless, alien and even cruel, the world turning on luck and fate rather than anything more constructive, all traces of a benign blueprint seemingly eroded.

I admit to an addiction to TV crime dramas and I am sometimes enticed by those stories that are serialized each night for a week. An example that sticks in my mind was called, quite simply, *Collision*. On a busy A-road in Essex there's a multiple pile-up and the story explores the lives of those caught up in the accident: who they were, what happened to them as a result, how they reacted and the impact on those close to them. Some die in the crash, some discover things about loved ones that they would never otherwise have known, an international scandal is uncovered and a young woman is prompted by the incident to fulfil a lifetime's ambition and travel the world.

The question running through the five episodes with an insistent tick, tick, tick is this: Why did this happen? Why then, why there? Why those people? The police have a theory about a Mr Norris, the man in the car at the front of the pile-up. They think that a triggered memory of something sinister in his life caused him to lose control of the vehicle, kick-starting the series of reactions that resulted in the multiple collision. But right at the very end of the last episode comes the prosaic answer. The accident happened because a wasp got into Mr Norris's car and while trying to swat it away he swerved, thus causing the chain of events that followed. And the chain of events that followed that. And that, and that.

There is a way of understanding life that sees God as entirely in control, micromanaging everything. Then there is a version that takes the implications of human freedom more seriously. Stuff happens and God does not intervene between cause and effect. Stuff happens because something else happened, and that happened because of something else. What happens may be tragic, destructive and incomprehensible. And there may be no reassuring explanation for the fact that at a particular moment in time we are caught up in particular events. It might just have been a wasp.

Yet there is another truth about life and our experience of the world that is intimately if paradoxically connected with this one and is the flipside of all that I've just said. If everything is caused by something else and we're all caught up in myriad chain reactions over which we have only minimal control, then ultimately everything connects with everything else, and that includes things that do seem to mean something as well as those that don't. Events and experiences may have threads that lead to others, helping us to orientate ourselves and to interpret what is happening. There are patterns, Fibonacci moments and exclamations of 'Yes, that makes sense: I recognize that from somewhere else.'

We live with these two truths. With this potent mix of what makes sense to us and what doesn't; with the causes that we can see and those that we cannot; with what reassures us and what rocks our boat; with repeated patterns that take our breath away in wonder, and seeming randomness that leaves us speechless with rage; with the things over which we have control and the things over which we do not; with what seems meaningless and what speaks powerfully of God's intimate love, the love that numbers each hair of our heads.[1] And ultimately it is as though we are told, 'This is the package. You can take it all or have none of it.'

The fact is that the world with which we are intimately engaged is not just miracle and beauty and the things that transport us with joy. It is war and poverty and filth and social injustice. Our hope is that in the depths as well as the elation we might navigate this gossamer web of potential connection and meaning in such a way that we live creative and positive lives, holding on to the instinct that ultimately our individual experiences might be part of a coherent whole, even if we will never achieve the helicopter view that would allow us to see it.

For a number of years I have been a contributor to BBC Radio 4's 'Thought for the Day'. There are other presenters who are much more savvy, incisive and simply knowledgeable in their theological reflection on political events, and the task of putting together a coherent 'Thought' can feel very daunting. But although I rarely have an incisive political line to take, I do feel the imperative to wrestle with the issues, to look for what truth the focus of the day might yield and to ask: what might there be in this that reveals something of God?

Part of belonging in the world is the opportunity to think about life beyond our own front door, to reflect on issues that other individuals face whether or not they are the same issues as ours, to direct our attention to what is happening in our nation and our global community as well as on our streets. This does not mean that we all need to be politicians, but we cannot pretend that what is happening to others is not in some sense also happening to us. To think about these things, even if we do not come up with definitive answers, increases our sense of belonging in the world, and our ability to make connections and discern patterns. We become a little more skilled at pulling gently at those threads of meaning that may enable us to make more sense of our own lives and, crucially, give life to our soul.

We will do this more successfully on some days than on others. There is a wonderful website called 'Platitude of the Day', which parodies every single 'Thought for the Day' and scores it out of five for 'platitudinousness'. My favourite parody of one of my own high-scoring contributions begins like this: 'Yesterday was the budget. Which brings me neatly on to the subject of spirituality.' Perhaps it had not been my finest two minutes and forty seconds on air! In trying to engage with the world beyond our front door, the connections that we make will on some occasions be more convincing than others. Making sense of human life is a complex, nuanced and messy process rather than an exact science or a method that can be learned from a textbook. But if our souls are to be open to a wider world than our immediate domestic situation we have to risk the messiness and mistakes in order to gain the pearl of great price, the discovery of God's presence in events, patterns and stories.

It probably helps us in these attempts if we are able to recover something of our childhood thirst to know the origin of all things. When our son, Joseph, was two years old he went through a phase of asking of absolutely everything, 'Where does it come from?' We were interrogated about the source of all that he saw and experienced. Where does this toy come from, where does nursery come from, where did I come from (answer: Mummy and Daddy made you – response, peals of laughter); where did the duck pond come from, where did teatime come from, and (while having his hair cut) where did my hair come from? It was a persistent and pretty unrelenting process, reflecting the human urge to discover a beginning and a significance for everything and therefore to understand it and mentally file it in its appropriate place. Joseph was paying attention, with an insatiable curiosity and interest, to everything around him and its connection with everything else.

Again, in *Strangely Warmed*, Andrew Rumsey reflects on the significance of sparrows. He calls the sparrow 'an icon of ordinary life, inlaid with the suggestion of God.'[2] This tiny feathered icon points both ways: towards the life of the earth and towards the divine, and is imbued with both, in the same way that the world is charged with sacred ordinariness. Jesus' presence in the world is the ultimate icon: God in the thick of things, wholly human, wholly divine, pointing both ways. When we look at Jesus we see human life lived as God intends, immersed in the miracle of being, fully reflecting God's glory, hallowing everything. And continually showing pointers to God: widows giving their final mite, mustard seeds, a woman searching for a lost coin, the lilies of the field and the birds of the air, perhaps particularly sparrows. All of these become ways of connecting with the life within life, the *nephesh* of God.

As someone who for four decades has been influenced by the Christian tradition my habit of mind is to relate my experience of the gossamer web of meaning and connection to my evolving understanding of God. Of course it is perfectly possible to relish the exquisite gifts of human existence without believing that those gifts might have a Source beyond themselves, that the gifts might have a Giver. Rumsey reflects on this as he muses on the biblical story of Creation: 'There is a strong possibility (proved correct after just two chapters) that humanity will opt not to return God's affection and, having been liberally showered with gifts like sex and summer fruits, might well choose to worship them instead.'[3]

I suspect, and I imagine that Rumsey does too, that God would rather we worshipped sex and summer fruits than not appreciate them at all! But to go one step further and rejoice in them as the happy result of Someone's creative genius is to begin to navigate the gossamer web which will inevitably involve interpreting the grit and agony of life as well as the sex and fruit.

The idea that all of creation, including ourselves, is imbued with the life of God and that this conviction might give us a handle on how to interpret our own lives may be a hunch that grows steadily in us from birth or overcomes us suddenly at a particular moment. For most of us it will wax and wane, as we waver between believing that human life and our own existence have coherence and meaning, and alternatively wondering whether in fact the complex construction of flesh and blood, bio-chemicals and neurological impulses that we undoubtedly are is *all* that we are, and is sufficient to account for everything that we feel, think and experience.

For many, the idea that the world in fact does make sense and the life within it connects profoundly with our own has involved particular moments along the way when something seemed to fall into place. Barbara Brown Taylor, an Episcopalian priest and professor of Christian spirituality in the United States, has written about the profound sense of connection with the world which began in her as a child when visiting what she thought of as a 'crystal stream' in a field near her home. But she goes on to say:

> Years later, I will discover that this was no crystal stream but a drainage ditch. The difference between these two descriptions of the same place will screw with my sense of reality for a long time. Is the Divine Presence in the world, or in my eye?[4]

Or is the Divine Presence both in the world and in our eye? I have a growing conviction that everything is sacred, especially the mundane, but that it takes a particular sort of looking, a particular approach and expectancy to see it. There is a sense in which we have to work at the connections in order to make a meaningful life for ourselves. This is not to say that meaning is unreal or illusory, just that it does not always appear on the surface of things, packaged and readily accessible. Meaning is real but it requires our engagement and interpretation in order to become real to us.

In the third chapter of John's Gospel there is a strange conversation between Christ and a man named Nicodemus. Nicodemus is interested in signs and when we encounter him in this story he is undoubtedly on to something about Jesus. He's been watching him, noticing, interpreting, questioning and paying attention to this extraordinary man. 'No one', he says, 'can do these signs that you do apart from the presence of God.'[5]

And off Jesus goes with a wonderfully enigmatic and powerful mixed metaphor, which is one minute about birth and the next minute about the direction of the wind:

> What is born of the flesh is flesh, and what is born of the Spirit is spirit. Do not be astonished that I said to you, 'You must be born from above.' The wind blows where it chooses, and you hear the sound of it, but you do not know where it comes from or where it goes. So it is with everyone who is born of the Spirit.

At the end of which, Nicodemus, not surprisingly, says something like, 'Well what will *that* look like, then?' And Jesus replies, 'If I have told you about earthly things and you do not believe, how can you believe if I tell you about heavenly things?'[6] In other words, you have to learn a different way of interpreting what you see.

Giving ourselves the best chance to make sense of the world and to discover God's presence in the DNA of life demands that we engage at all levels with new experiences and ideas and look with fresh eyes at the most familiar things. As Roald Dahl urges in his story *The Minpins*, 'watch with glittering eyes the whole world around you because the greatest secrets are always hidden in the most unlikely places. Those who don't believe in magic will never find it.'[7]

There is a poem that captures beautifully the vulnerability, the commitment and the occasional eureka moment that characterize this openness of soul that I am trying to describe. It is by Don Paterson and it is called 'Why do you stay up so late?'

> *Why do you stay up so late?*
>
> I'll tell you, if you really want to know:
> remember that day you lost two years ago
> at the rockpool where you sat and played the jeweller
> with all those stones you'd stolen from the shore?
> Most of them went dark and nothing more,
> but sometimes one would blink the secret colour
> it had locked up somewhere in its stony sleep.
> This is how you knew the ones to keep.
>
> So I collect the dull things of the day
> in which I see some possibility
> but which are dead and which have the surprise
> I don't know, and I've no pool to help me tell –
> so I look at them and look at them until
> one thing makes a mirror in my eyes
> then I paint it with the tear to make it bright.
> This is why I sit up through the night.[8]

That loving attentiveness to the stones from a rock pool, coupled with the willingness to bathe them in the salt water of tears, is a wonderful image of what we might do with the stuff of everyday life. The fragile web of patterns and connections can easily be ripped apart by our experiences of rejection and disappointment. Yet in all of our projects and dreams there is the potential to discover the life of God under the skin of the world, pointing to the significance, meaning and purpose of our own lives.

When we try to do this consistently throughout the days, months and years, we are increasing in ourselves the capacity to feel and experience God in our bodies, our relationships and the opportunities of our lives; in 'the person coming around the corner, the moment of stillness, the peace in pain';[9] in summer fruit and sex, but also in the difficult places. In times of contentment, when we feel at home in the world; yet also, as we will see in Chapter 6, in times when we feel anything but sure of ourselves.

Mark Oakley, Canon Treasurer at St Paul's Cathedral, has suggested that 'God is in the world as poetry is in the poem'.[10] It is a subtle and persistent process to immerse our stones in the pool and discover what they might reveal of the God whose presence in the world cannot be separated out and examined any more than our soul can be divided from the totality of our human life. But it is a way of living that slowly and surely expands that soul, enlarging our capacity to connect courageously with all that we encounter in the human life around us and the complexities of our global community, both when the correlations and connections are elusive and when they are tantalizingly present, as nature offers the spiral of a seashell, the pattern of a pine cone, and the exquisitely unfolding fern by way of hints and gestures towards the divine presence within.

6

Down the stairs backwards
Does anyone else feel this vulnerable?

My friend Rachel attended a funeral that happened to be held in her old church, a place in which she had formerly been very involved for over 20 years. Having realized that her soul was longing for a different space in which to explore life, one that more fully reflected her current thinking and believing, she had quietly taken leave of that community about 18 months' earlier. She described how odd and exposing it felt to be back among so many people who had known her in a very different phase and whose lives were still shaped by her old way of seeing things.

This sense of exposure was only increased by the fact that the occasion was a funeral, with the inevitable salutary reminders that in the end we are all stripped of our accomplishments and accoutrements and stand before God utterly undressed. Nowhere to hide, even if we wanted to. Describing her sense of the occasion a few days later Rachel wrote to a friend:

> Of course, each person there experienced it in a uniquely personal way, and you couldn't help but be conscious of that. I'm still feeling rather too much a week on – so many faces from the past and memories evoked – though the deep time concept[1] is helping me see that I can celebrate the past as if it were as immediate as the present, and that the future is somehow enfolding me even now, in a friendly manner, and is certainly not something to be feared.

We went on to talk about the efforts that we all make to try to appear invulnerable; to give the impression that we've got it all together, are happy, fulfilled, in control, productive, grown-up. We are flattered when others tell us that we appear that way. One of the other school-gate mothers once said to me, 'I didn't realize that you have *three* children – and you always look so glamorous and calm!' I laughed like a drain, thinking of the mornings that I lurch out of the house considerably later than intended, having yelled at the children for not being ready on time, not a trace of make-up on my face and wearing whatever is closest to hand.

We love to appear invulnerable, calm and omni-competent. Yet deep in our souls don't we all recognize that it is often when people are at their most fragile that they connect most fully with one another? That there is an attraction about each other's vulnerability because in it we recognize another human being in all of his or her giftedness and brokenness, a real person with whom we can engage and identify and have a creative and sustaining relationship? It is through the honesty of admitting a dependence on alcohol that members of Alcoholics Anonymous are able to be a real resource to one another in their lifelong efforts to conquer their addiction. Without the courage to do this they struggle on alone, without the deep friendship and support that could have transformed their lives.

We are afraid of exposing our brokenness to others because in doing so we open ourselves to ridicule, misunderstanding or criticism. Yet if we have the courage to be metaphorically and appropriately naked with each other it opens up the possibility of so much learning and connecting; so much growth for our soul. This is the way that strength lies: not in the ability to appear invulnerable. We can spend a lifetime valiantly soldering the cracks in our armour but what we end up with, invincible though it may appear, will inevitably be misshapen and unreal. We may also be very lonely inside our cast-iron shell.

The Buddhist teacher Pema Chödrön has said that 'when we touch the centre of sorrow, when we sit with discomfort without trying to fix it, when we stay present to the pain of disapproval or betrayal and let it soften us, those are the times that we connect with *bodhichitta*': that is, the most real part of us; that part that is undefended by the habit of pretending to ourselves that we feel okay; the part that refuses to reinforce itself against the admission of vulnerability, to batten down the hatches or to ignore the suffering of others; the part that instead chooses to respond with deep honesty and courage.

Again Chödrön tells us:

> Affirmations are like screaming that you're okay in order to overcome this whisper that you're not. That is a big contrast to actually uncovering the whisper . . . and moving closer to all those edgy feelings that maybe you're not okay. Well, no big deal. None of us is okay and all of us are fine. It's not just one way. We are walking, talking, paradoxes.[2]

We survive and grow because we devise strategies to live with our fragility, rather than pretending that it is not there. If you can admit to your crippling shyness you can begin to find ways to manage social situations. If you pretend it isn't a problem you risk gaining a reputation for being brusque, brittle or just downright unfriendly.

The late Michael Mayne, formerly Dean of Westminster Abbey, told of his experience of suffering from ME in a book called *A Year Lost and Found*. When it was published a colleague asked, 'Do you enjoy undressing in public?' The remark spoke volumes about the other person, who presumably would rather have died a thousand deaths than risk their own nakedness and vulnerability. Yet Mayne claimed that he had more responses to that book than to anything else that he had ever written.[3] People connect more fully with an admission of fragility than an assertion of strength.

Many of us will remember our mothers' advice that we should always wear good underwear in case we are caught up in an accident and find our dignity exposed! Thinking about nakedness and vulnerability makes me wonder what the equivalent of good underwear might be as we seek to be more self-revealing in order to connect with others. I guess that good underwear might be the ability to discern the difference between appropriately sharing our innermost thoughts with people who have the potential to empathize and understand, and randomly sharing too much detail with strangers or those easily embarrassed by the intimacies of others.

There is also the question of timing: good underwear might be a metaphor for the ability to discern the appropriate moments in which to let down our guard. Or we might hold close to ourselves, as a beautiful piece of lingerie, the reassurance of God's connection with our fragility; the belief that in the very heart of the divine we find nakedness and vulnerability and brokenness.

The gospel story that speaks most directly to me about brokenness and exposure is that of the two disciples who have an unexpected encounter with the risen Christ as they journey together out of Jerusalem shortly after the events of Good Friday. One is called Cleopas, the other is quite probably his wife, who had been present at the crucifixion.[4] Luke tells us: 'Now on that same day two of them were going to a village called Emmaus, about seven miles from Jerusalem, and talking with each other about all these things that had happened.'[5] These friends of Jesus take a long walk out of the city, mulling over the violent and disorientating events in which they have been caught up. Probably they were trying to make some sense of it, to see a pattern, to find reassurance that it meant something. And they would undoubtedly be wondering what it meant for their own lives. As they walk, alongside them appears someone whom they assume to be a stranger, and when he asks them 'What are you discussing? . . . What things?', it all comes spilling out.

'We had this amazing leader', they say, 'who was a fantastic prophet, but then our religious leaders handed him over to be crucified. It was barbaric and terrifying and we can't get the images out of our minds. It seemed like it was all over but the most bizarre thing is that some of our friends say he's still alive.' The subtext of all this: we thought our lives were sorted, that we'd found meaning and purpose and inspiration, but it's all fallen apart now, it's broken, we are in a mess, vulnerable, exposed, frightened and none of it makes sense.

Later in the story the travellers decide to take rooms in an inn for the night, and they invite the stranger to join them. I'm always struck by the fact that it was when Jesus was in the act of breaking something that the scales fell from his friends' eyes and at last they recognized him. Not when he questioned them, not when he explained the Scriptures to them, not when he accepted their invitation to come and eat and stay the night with them, but when he tore open the bread and offered it to them, in all its brokenness; then and only then were their minds broken open to see and understand and know that this ordinary stranger, this very human companion, is in fact the risen Christ; only then did they sense the possibility of rediscovering some meaning for their lives. Had they not opened their hearts and minds to him in the nakedness of honest vulnerability, this might never have happened.

Among other things, this story reveals that God is fully present as our companion not only in the good and easy times, but when we are at our lowest ebb; that perhaps it is even in the experience of brokenness that we are able most fully to identify with the God who was willingly and unreservedly broken as an inevitable consequence of being here among us. We are able to get up and carry on with life because we have seen that there is tragedy at the heart of God that mirrors the reality of the tragedies at the heart of our own lives.

There will be many reasons why we identify with the sense of disorientation and disbelief that overwhelmed those two friends of Jesus. The ground can suddenly sink beneath us as the result of acute financial problems or the sudden impossibility of communicating with a teenage child who was such an easy and close confidante throughout childhood. The journalist Victoria Coren speaks of her incapacitating vulnerability in the face of her father's life-threatening illness.

I am not ready for my father to die ... I have been frightened of this for my entire life and I hoped I would be ready when it happened, but I am not. I cannot bear this to be now. I have never been so scared or so sad ... I believe in God. I have always believed in God. I tried not to, but I do ... I tell God, every day, that I am not ready for this.[6]

Our vulnerability and our sense of exposure can be terrifying. The acute sense of our own shakiness is not something to be deliberately contrived in a masochistic attempt to speed up our learning about life. But when it comes upon us it sometimes proves to be a fast-track to enlarging our souls. Many people who know their own fragility will tell us that it brings a much greater understanding of themselves and others. It seems to be in the nature of human life, or at least an experience which many people have, that the wilderness periods teach them the greatest, if hardest-won, lessons. They also leave an imprint on our soul that enables more profound connections with other people.

According to those who knew him as a child, from a very early age my father had a habit of sitting on his trike, looking into the middle distance, not seeming to be doing anything. When asked what he was up to, he would say, 'I'm doing my thinking.' And much of his thinking, it seemed, centred on God. At the age of five he announced that what he wanted to be was a priest. He never wavered from that pronouncement and this very early decision, the result of his infant 'thinking', shaped the entirety of his life.

But the empathy and compassion that later characterized his priestly ministry was, I believe, forged in the fire of his own wilderness experience. Having read theology at university and been accepted as a potential ordinand he went, at the tender age of 20, to theological college for his ministerial training. During his first year an incident born of naivety and misunderstanding caused the principal, motivated probably by self-protection, to write to my dad during the next summer holiday and request him not to return for his second year, or ever.

It was seven years before an understanding and sympathetic bishop agreed to sponsor my father to complete his theological training and be ordained. During those years he worked as a teacher, initially in Salford Docks in a school where to turn your back on the class was to risk your personal safety. He and my mother, long engaged, separated temporarily at some point during those years. The combination of circumstances was an intensely painful and formative wilderness, but in it were forged the embryonic grace and pastoral sensitivity that became such gifts to others.

The Christian faith embraces human fragility and the reality of our nakedness. Not in the sense of wallowing in all of this, but by encouraging us to live and work with the precarious nature of our physical, mental and spiritual well-being as finely tuned human beings, impressionable and sensitive to what happens to us. Which of course is the root of our strength.

As we learn to live with the ground having given way beneath our feet, it can help to know that we are all in this together. Lucy Winkett, Rector of St James's Piccadilly, describes the experience of sitting in front of Edvard Munch's painting *The Scream*. She says:

> I spent hours in front of this painting in Oslo National Art Gallery one cold afternoon in November. The fact that my own heart was breaking found expression and a home in the figure in the fore-ground, crouched over while everyone else walked on by. It wasn't at all depressing – I was not driven into deeper despair, quite the opposite. Somehow I was understood, the burden became bearable and I was able to walk back onto the street.[7]

As we share the broken bread among ourselves we know the truth of God's presence in one another in all of our brokenness. When we know others to have unmet longings like ours or to live with equally debilitating pain, because we see God broken and torn apart yet somehow gloriously still God, the breaking of our own hearts finds some sort of comfort and we can find the resources within ourselves to carry on.

In what sense everything will be okay we rarely know. But we start to learn to live with the brokenness and vulnerability. Yes we are fragile, frail, psychologically and physically, but we are also okay. We're surviving. We're more than surviving. We're nurtured and held and encouraged and loved by a God of infinite patience and compassion. We are creative and surprising and tenacious and bold, and in our state of being broken open we are learning what it is to risk being naked to one another.

If we admit and acknowledge our vulnerability to one another this can sometimes shake and stir us into opening up our lives to questions about why and who we are and what we are for, questions that we may answer more fully and wisely if we have the courage to share our stories and to draw on one another's experience as well as our own.

Acknowledging our fragility, even helplessness at times, does not mean coming to a standstill, being frozen for ever in that moment. It is the beginning of being healed, whatever that might mean in the circumstances of our lives. It will rarely mean returning to our previous state, miraculously unscathed by our experiences. Neither will it mean remaining as we are, paralysed by our wounds. As a teenager a song by Martyn Joseph taught me that 'Broken wings don't always heal to fly'. I knew the truth of the words without having had the experience, but ten years later I knew the experience too. Being healed but not to fly meant that I couldn't put the clock back and avoid the damage of a failed marriage. It will mean all sorts of things to different people: having to live with permanently diminished energy after a debilitating illness, or to accept that the longed-for promotion has passed us by. While recognizing that the scars will stay we can refuse to be paralysed by the experience. We can move on.

There is something in all of this that relies on our ability to let go, just as we are learning to do through the stages and transitions of life. We have to let go of our illusion that we are in control of much at all; of our desire to mould other people in our own image; of dreams that cannot, for whatever reason, be fulfilled; of the past.

Mike Riddell gives us the salutary advice, 'It is wisdom indeed to let go of that which cannot be held, and to hold on to that which cannot be lost.'[8] It is wisdom indeed, but it is a very hard lesson to grasp.

Emma Forrest describes this process of being healed but not to fly, of giving up on our image of ourselves as having got it all together, and in doing so learning the merits of taking things step by step. While she was in the process of recovering from a mental breakdown, she and her cats moved from an apartment to a house. There, Junior, the younger and less confident cat, has to learn to negotiate the stairs. He is terrified of this process and at night has to be carried down to his litter tray every time he needs to use it, until eventually there is a minor breakthrough. Forrest writes:

> One night I wake hearing rustling. I peer over the banister and see Junior in his box. From then on we never discuss anything, but he can do it. It's like getting well. You do it how you can do it, so long as it's getting done, you're OK. He comes downstairs backwards like how one might manoeuvre out of a tree.[9]

In some phases of our lives 'down the stairs backwards' is pretty much the only way we can do it. But we are not alone. How much more do people reflect the empathy and compassion of the crucified God when they are able to admit their vulnerability, to acknowledge how fragile their life is, to offer to their family, their friends, their colleagues, their community, all that they are and not just the bits that they want people to see?

It is then that we are able to take our experiences of brokenness and weave them into our lives. Whatever we have faced and dealt with becomes, strangely, a gift to others in their helplessness and part of the gradual and sometimes painful unfolding and maturing of our own soul. We wish that it did not have to be this way but the nature of this life is such that we learn most through our fragility. Brokenness and the experiences that it brings become our strength, perhaps even our way to resurrection.

I have a friend who in her late teens had a malignant lymphoma and survived. It has left her vulnerable, however, to other forms of cancer, and at the age of 50 she was diagnosed with another cancer in one of her breasts. Her decision was to have a preventive double mastectomy. Following the surgery and breast reconstruction, her old bras no longer fitted and she decided to do something creative with them.

Among other things, Ali is an artist who particularly enjoys working with fabric. So out of that now-redundant lingerie she created the most amazing art quilt. She sees this as a way of celebrating her past, what she has been, bringing it into the present and what she is, and taking it forward into the future, what she will be. She now offers to make similar artistic pieces for others and runs workshops to encourage them to create their own, whether they are weaving their late father's old ties into a cushion cover or their old bras into a lacy wall hanging!

The works of Brart[10] (as Ali's initiative is appropriately called) created out of these experiences speak of beauty, pain and transformation. They celebrate sheer human tenacity in the face of tragedy and loss. They bring meaning to the most challenging of human circumstances because they evoke strength in weakness, and the possibility, against all odds, of rising up again. They remind us of the importance, the usefulness and even the beauty of good underwear. They celebrate the ability to be fragile in one another's presence in a way that enables greater human connection and creates a challenging and life-giving space in which, with courage, the soul can learn, flourish and be renewed.

7

'Never fully known, never properly kissed'
Am I happy enough?

———◆———

Martin Seligman is not, by nature, a particularly cheerful person. Yet he is the author of *Authentic Happiness*,[1] a bestseller that established him as something of a happiness guru. The key to this seeming contradiction is Seligman's idea that whether or not we are naturally upbeat it is possible to maximize our happiness by taking certain conscious and deliberate steps. The popularity of the book and its follow-up, *Flourish*,[2] bears witness to the innate human desire for happiness and the fact that many people consciously pursue pleasure as a goal: if we are reading a book about it then presumably we are not yet happy enough and we would like that to change.

In these two books Seligman charts something of a journey in his thinking. In the first he identifies three ways of increasing our levels of happiness, focused on the ideas of positive emotion, authentic gratification and finding meaning through serving a purpose beyond ourselves. In *Flourish* he expands upon his original suggestions and uses the acronym PERMA to list the key ways in which we might work towards flourishing: positive emotion, engagement, relationships, meaning and accomplishment.

He also reveals his discomfort that after he wrote the first book the word happiness was hijacked to mean something more superficial than he had intended. He cites a weakness in his previous research, saying that when people are questioned about their happiness their response tends to reflect their mood at the time rather than their more deep-seated levels of contentment. In identifying these issues Seligman puts his finger squarely on the pulse of the happiness debate and identifies a key conundrum: what is the core nature of this happiness that we are pursuing with such determination? Will we know it when we find it? Can we trust it to stay? Put another way, is happiness merely the emotion we experience when we are having a good time, a feeling that can be here one minute, gone the next? Or, in the depth of our being, are we actually longing for something more deep-seated and less vulnerable to the vicissitudes of our circumstances, hormones and emotions?

If you have a nagging sense that you are not as happy as you might be, Seligman has some interesting ideas about how you might encourage the right conditions in your life for happiness to emerge. He belongs to the school of thought known as Positive Psychology, which is far more interested in building on our existing strengths than examining and addressing our brokenness, anger, grief, or any other difficult experience. Others who think in this vein are Professor Richard Layard who heads up the Wellbeing Programme at LSE's Centre for Economic Performance, and Mark Williamson, who has the enviable job title 'Director of the Action for Happiness Movement'.

My take on all of this would be that for the flourishing of the *nephesh* or life force within us, for the healthy growth of our soul, we need to acknowledge and address both sets of experiences and emotions: the negative and the positive. This chapter is therefore followed by one that explores the experiences associated with human angst, unhappiness and what we have come to call depression. But I do believe that those who are looking at ideas around happiness, flourishing and well-being have much to offer as we learn to nurture our soul.

One idea that Seligman explores is the concept of 'flow'. Flow is what we experience when we are wholly focused and fully absorbed in what we are doing. It is characterized by 'being one with the music, time stopping, and the loss of self-consciousness'.[3]

We probably know how this feels. People experience flow in widely different contexts: you might know it through playing a particular sport, or perhaps when you are creating some sort of work of art. Flow leads to happiness. Flow is about being present with the whole of our being, rather than just physically in the room. It means paying full attention to whatever we are doing and whoever we are with.

There are many things that come between us and the potential for sheer, simple enjoyment; things that stop us from being unself-consciously happy. One of the biggest issues is our inability to be wholly in one place at any one time. People speak of living in the present moment and how difficult this can be. We do have a habit of allowing ourselves to be split: body here, thoughts there; physic-ally in the present, mentally in the past; alongside people, but longing to be alone; solitary, yet longing to be in a crowd.

This habit of being less than fully present can undermine our enjoyment of where and who we are and it can frustrate our relationships. It may at its worst engender a sort of dissection of the soul, as the life within us becomes fragmented, distracted and unfocused.

Occasionally those close to us might pull us up on this, perhaps because we have brought our laptop to bed or arrived for coffee with a friend and immediately taken a call on our mobile from someone else.

One day our daughter Olivia was chatting away in seemingly unstoppable fashion when she halted mid-sentence to exclaim, 'Mum, listen to me!' 'I am listening to you,' I said, somewhat dishonestly. 'No you're not,' she said, 'You're *un*-listening to me.' She was right. Part of me was listening but part of my attention was very definitely elsewhere. I wasn't fully present to her or to what she was trying to share with me. I was neglecting Olivia and our conversation, to the detriment of our time together.

We all un-listen at times to people, to situations and to events. There are many reasons that we might do this: overload, anxiety, boredom, tiredness, the desire to avoid becoming involved where we don't really want to be. We can also fail fully to appreciate the most precious and obvious riches of our lives simply because we allow day-to-day irritations to make us grumpy. I was reminded of this in the local DVD shop during a brief exchange with the young Arab man behind the counter. Annoyed with myself for caving in to pressure and buying an expensive copy of the latest Disney release I said irritably, 'I'll never be rich with three children.' 'But that is why you *are* rich', came the gentle but insistent reply.

There is a certain urgency about our need to pay attention to the people and things immediately around us, to learn to be wholly alive and present to the moment, to stop in our tracks to notice the smallest things that bring joy. This is about learning to rejoice in and appreciate what we have before it grows up and leaves home, or merges into winter, or becomes something that we could do in the past that is no longer possible for us as we have moved almost imperceptibly into another stage of life. The simple fact is that although we can enjoy planning ahead, and undoubtedly we can be sustained by rich memories of previous years, happiness is like pain: we can only feel it in the present. This is the only time and place where it has the power to touch us deeply.

In our most holy and connected moments we know the truth that God is to be found right here and now. When we experience the sudden quick conviction of God's presence through another person, a piece of music or a great game of football, because we see a kingfisher or a glorious city skyline, either way we experience it in that instant, together with the deep surge of happiness that brings. But much of the time we are looking the other way, backwards or forwards, ahead or to the side, missing that opportunity to lock eyes and engage our souls with what is on offer in the present.

One of the reasons that we struggle to live our lives in the present is that they are both enhanced and challenged by the miracle of twenty-first-century gadgetry. This means that we are often to be found negotiating between the enjoyment of what we are doing and the impulse to record it. I know this struggle well because

I am our family's official photographer and camcorder operator, responsible for preserving the best memories as images to be revisited again and again in the future. So it is that I am frequently urged to 'Take a picture, take a picture', when all that I really want to do is enjoy the moment without having to look at it through a lens and consider the best composition, frame and lighting for the subject.

The journalist Jemima Kiss talks about this dilemma when she describes a magical moment on an early morning walk. It happened to take place during a weekend when she had resolved to eschew all communications devices and recording gadgetry. Glimpsing the breathtaking sight of a barn owl in flight, Kiss reflects:

> Ordinarily, my next thought would have been to pull out my phone and take a photo, send a tweet or record a video. Tweeting is like breathing and photos and video have documented nearly every day of my 21-month-old son's life . . . my enjoyment split between that technological impulse and the more delicate human need to be in the moment. This is how we live.[4]

She is right. It is how we live. Or how we sometimes less-than-live, because it leads to such fragmentation of our focus that we are all over the place and unable to occupy and enjoy the moment. Unless we are really there we can't be fully touched by the joy of the present experience. Our soul cannot absorb what is on offer, what we might learn or enjoy, other than here and now.

There is a difference, though, between being fully present to ourselves and engaging in an unhelpful measuring exercise, obsessively assessing our level of happiness on an invisible gauge. All the joy can leach from an occasion or conversation if we are constantly monitoring whether or not it is making us as happy as it could. In an excellent debate on the subject of happiness, held at St Paul's Cathedral, one of the cathedral clergy, Mark Oakley, suggested that we seem unable to consider ourselves happy unless we are being seen to be happy and can see ourselves that way. So unless our social lives are documented and publicized on Facebook and we can see ourselves there and know that others are seeing us, looking radiant and carefree, we are not fully convinced that our happiness is real. It is not enough to enjoy ourselves, we need to be seen to be enjoying ourselves, preferably to be enjoying ourselves more than everyone else![5]

This illustrates something about the elusive nature of happiness and our sometimes inappropriate attempts to capture it in aspic. Again Mark Oakley puts it beautifully: 'This word happiness is a flirt . . . always, as it were, on the pull. But when you go to the bar to buy it a drink you return to find it gone. Never fully known, never properly kissed.'[6] Happiness is quirky. It can slip through our hands because we are trying to hold on to it too tightly, yet it often overcomes us, unbidden and unlooked for, in moments when we are least expecting it. Afterwards we can't always work out exactly why it did suddenly well up in us. It could have been for the smallest of reasons: the smile of a complete stranger as a tangential human connection is accidentally made, the sudden sense of freedom on a day off, falling inexplicably in love once again with someone we've loved for a long time. A flood of well-being can overwhelm us when we least expect it.

There is a sudden *joie de vivre* that is wonderful when it happens but cannot really be planned into our lives or cultivated. The elusive nature of happiness accords with the elusive possibility of a concrete description and the lack of a formula to guarantee our hold on it. It just happens when we are not looking. If we are alone we can have the oddest of responses: we laugh aloud, or in my case find myself sliding deliberately, adolescently and somewhat precariously down the length of our polished wooden hallway in my somewhat-surprised fleecy socks.

I should confess that I have a Facebook page and think that in some ways it is a very good social tool, but perhaps another peril of being part of the Facebook generation is the undermining sense that we all need to look for happiness in the same places: seemingly at parties and on the wrong side of several beers. The words of Mark Williamson of the Action for Happiness movement are pertinent here:

> there is evidence that we are quite bad at knowing what makes us happy. We are bombarded by the media and marketing messages that success is about fame or wealth, although this is often the route to misery . . . We need to be honest with ourselves and resist what peer groups and society tell us is the right answer.[7]

We are vastly different human beings who find joy and contentment in a myriad of different ways. I know a married couple whose on-going and creative debate about how to live their lives and spend their time is shaped by their different instincts regarding where they might find enjoyment and stimulation. Ruth is always up for the next adventure, the next travel opportunity, the next challenge at work. She loves meeting new people and experiencing things she hasn't encountered before. She has a job that takes her far and wide into situations that are extraordinarily different from what she finds at home. Her partner, Andrew, relishes what is familiar and cherishes what is beautiful and precious in the so-called ordinary things of life. Meeting with long-loved friends, going to favourite places, at work the enjoyment of familiar tasks completed well, and then weekends spent luxuriating in freedom, not having to be driven and timetabled.

Their debate is along the lines: is happiness to be found in the everyday or the extraordinary? Andrew might argue that the extraordinary is to be found right under our noses in what we had assumed was ordinary. Ruth would always go for things new, the different culture, the more obviously extraordinary experience. Neither of them is right or wrong. Happiness lies, potentially, in both directions – as may discontentment! But it helps us to know, as we accumulate experience and understanding of ourselves, the directions in which we are most likely to find it.

The closest that Jesus comes to a discussion or exploration of happiness is, perhaps, found in Matthew and Luke and has become known as the Beatitudes. Luke tells us that Jesus has been up a mountain praying all night. Then 'He came down with them and stood on a level place'. It is significant that he levelled with them. This was important teaching, ideas which might, if they took them seriously, radically change their lives. This is what follows:

> Then [Jesus] looked up at his disciples and said:
> 'Blessed are you who are poor,
>   for yours is the kingdom of God.
> 'Blessed are you who are hungry now,
>   for you will be filled.
> 'Blessed are you who weep now,
>   for you will laugh.
> 'Blessed are you when people hate you, and when they exclude you, revile you, and defame you on account of the Son of Man. Rejoice on that day and leap for joy, for surely your reward is great in heaven; for that is what their ancestors did to the prophets.'

These blessings, sounding somewhat unattractive in parts, with any gratification being delayed until another life, are followed by a series of woes:

> 'But woe to you who are rich,
>   for you have received your consolation.
> 'Woe to you who are full now,
>   for you will be hungry.
> 'Woe to you who are laughing now,
>   for you will mourn and weep.
> 'Woe to you when all speak well of you, for that is what their ancestors did to the false prophets.'[8]

Jesus inverts our expectations and in doing so underlines something that we have already realized: happiness is not necessarily to be found where we expect it. And what we find might, in fact, not feel like happiness. But we will know that it is something approaching contentment for the way that it grounds and steadies us, roots us in reality. We do not tend to expect poverty or persecution to bring a sense of blessing. Conversely we assume that riches and certainly laughter are an indication of life satisfaction. In bringing all of these things into surprising juxtaposition Jesus is refusing to engage with a superficial version of happiness. He pushes us deeper into our exploration of what joy, happiness and contentment might really mean.

Often when we find happiness it is not because we were consciously engaged in its pursuit. In other words, you can't really cultivate it; rather, it comes as a by-product of something else. Hope and tragedy are intimately interwoven in the lives of many people, as they are fundamentally ingrained in the created world. And so the nineteenth-century French novelist Stendhal makes the following quite startling observations, which go to the heart of the happiness debate:

> The happy few ... are those who remain emotionally alive, who never compromise, who never succumb to cynicism or the routine of the second-hand. The happy few are not necessarily happy. But they are never corrupted and seldom bored. The happy few possess what Baudelaire called 'impeccable *naiveté*,' the ability to see the world always afresh, either in its tragedy or its hope.[9]

Happiness is incidental rather than something to be pursued and comes upon us when we are being what we are meant to be, doing what we most like to do, with the people who most energize and nurture us. We will create in our lives the conditions for happiness by discovering the path that we are supposed to tread, and walking it with a sense of hope and expectation, and openness to wherever it might take us and whatever we might learn along the way. As we do this God longs for us to delight in one another and in the world. In order to do that we have to deal with our demons. None of this will guarantee our happiness, but it will give us the best chance to flourish, and the sudden welling up within ourselves of an unbidden and very precious joy is often a consequence of such flourishing.

Our daughter Olivia became obsessed a while ago by the question of how she might know that she is alive. We tried many different ways of helping her to resolve this issue and eventually settled on the reality of her heartbeat. It was one clue that Olivia really seemed to trust. She would place her hand on her chest to feel that heartbeat, and as long as the thud, thud, thud vibrated against her small palm she was happy and reassured. She quite literally listened to her heart in order to know that she was alive. Happiness is something about staying in touch with our heartbeat. To know that we are happy we need to stay in touch with that rhythm, with what keeps us alive, engaged and wanting to be here.

Happiness is complicated! The pursuit of it is not nearly so simple as avoiding all that is negative and damaging. Few of us can spend all of our time doing lovely things that make us feel warm and fuzzy. Happiness requires us to integrate all the different aspects of ourselves: the good, the bad and the ugly. If we are unable to do this there will always be things threatening to emerge from the undergrowth of our fragile pleasure: issues that we haven't dealt with, people with whom we have an uneasy truce, triggers that cause us to respond in a way that we ourselves don't expect. If happiness is to be rooted and grounded in our lives in such a way that it might nurture our soul, we now need to look at how we deal with the difficult stuff too.

8

The rawness of peeled carrots
How do we deal with depression?

———•••——

Western society has learnt the stark lesson in recent years that a large number of people feel very unhappy at some point in their lives. I am not talking here of the sort of unhappiness that overwhelms us in response to a specific event, but a more general state of mind that we refer to as anxiety or depression. Opinions vary considerably on whether there is 'more of it about' than there used to be. There might be. Or it could just be that we understand it a bit better and talk of it a little more openly. When I was a child the phrase was, 'She's bad with her nerves, you know.' A different way of putting it, but the same experience.

Giles Andreae is a writer, poet and artist who is known to many by his pseudonym, Purple Ronnie. Over the years many amusing and slightly dodgy poems have flowed from that source and been reproduced on fridge magnets, mugs and birthday cards. His other persona, Edward Monkton, aims his wisdom primarily at women. In word and line drawings he celebrates such things as the power of high heels and the life-saving properties of chocolate. Andreae is clearly a man with a keen eye for the nuances of human life and a great sense of humour.

Yet in 2009 he had a sudden, unexpected and crushing experience of depression that left him utterly devastated. A year later he wrote:

I remember once, as a child, peeling carrots for a family meal, and I found myself wondering what on earth it must feel like to be one of those carrots. Yes, now I know. When you have depression you feel as violated as if you have just been peeled – and you're standing naked in the wind. It is as visceral and as peculiar as that.[1]

Depression overcomes some people often, others seldom and many at some time or another. It occurs on a spectrum: some people suffer it in its mildest form, some live with its most chronic and debilitating effects, many hover in between. Seemingly striking anyone at any time, depression can bring fear and fragility, self-doubt and a sudden inability to deal creatively with the big questions of life. The power of this experience to destroy people's happiness and sense of meaning is considerable.

Depression has an impact not only on the sufferers but on those around them. If you have a close family member, partner, friend or colleague who suffers from depression it is highly likely that to a certain extent you have been stopped in your own tracks by the reverberations. To see someone you love, admire, or have always assumed to be on top of things now deadened to human relating, untouched by the events of the world, losing the desire to live, is to say the least a very hard thing to handle.

The experience of depression threatens relationships, families, hope and our grasp on meaningful human relating. It leaves us wondering where the person we knew went to, why we cannot bring him or her back, how it can be that he or she appears to have no desire to return to us. However much we understand about the condition and the utter impossibility of sufferers pulling themselves up out of the black hole by their own bootstraps, it is hard to be on the receiving end of what looks like utter indifference.

My friend in America, having just given birth, told me that when she rang her mother in the UK with the news, 'She responded as though I was telling her that we'd just bought a bag of carrots.' Suffering from severe clinical depression at the time, the new grandmother had no way of accessing a more appropriate response to the news, and neither could her daughter avoid the hurt her response evoked.

There is a wide spectrum of experiences that might be described as depression and a vast range of opinion on how to treat or handle it. Some would argue that depression is primarily accounted for by biochemical imbalances that are treatable with medication. In fact there are certain conditions of the mind that are so distressing and unstable that for the well-being of the person concerned and the safety of those around them there seems no other possible response, at least in the first instance, than medical intervention. There are also, however, many people who are aware of their own anxiety, unhappiness and mental disease and choose to turn to therapeutic solutions.

Whatever the cause of an individual's particular depression and whatever the possible sources of healing, it tends to be a very specific and focused experience of human fragility. It answers the ultimate question, 'What is the point of life?' with a resounding silence. It leaches life of meaning. And in the words of Richard Rohr, 'We can live without success, but the soul cannot live without meaning.'[2] How the soul rediscovers that meaning is the most poignant question for those who have lost their hold on it. What seems clear is that it is extremely difficult to think our way back to a meaningful life, at least on our own. Depression responds with a hollow laugh when told to pull itself together.

There is a story in the Gospels of a woman who for 12 years has suffered from chronic bleeding[3] and has spent all of her financial resources trying to find a cure. As Jesus is on his way to a man's sick daughter, accompanied by a large crowd, the woman struggles through the throng and touches the hem of his garment. Her bleeding made her ritually unclean, so to be present in the crowd at all was to risk social embarrassment and acute rejection, but she was desperate. Luke tells us, 'She came up behind him and touched the fringe of his clothes, and immediately her haemorrhage stopped. Then Jesus asked, "Who touched me? . . . Someone touched me; for I noticed that power had gone out from me."'[4]

Most people need a source of help and healing if, in the face of depression, they are to begin to recover their sense of life as having any purpose or meaning. Sometimes the depression itself prevents them from connecting with that source of help, so debilitating is it that to risk venturing out into the crowd is simply not an option. Then others have to do this on the sufferer's behalf.

The sufferer has to be led to the place where he or she needs to be, or to the person or people who can best help.

Depression is so utterly life-sapping, so haemorrhaging of our sense of purpose, that anything we can do to ensure our own mental health and that of those around us, we should do. There are things that we can put in place, none of which are magical talismans, but they may help us to keep in touch with our sense of life as meaningful and positive. We can ensure that we eat well, sleep well, look after our physical health and fitness; that we allow ourselves time out and mental space. We can build the life-giving relationships that bring us joy and engage in the activities that give us satisfaction. We can go to the places that energize us and we can be prepared to admit our vulnerability.

The campaigner, psychotherapist and writer Susie Orbach has suggested that mental equilibrium lies 'not in the dissolving of confusion, sorrow, muddle, rage and despair but the recognition of its legitimacy'. She explains that people need to find words to describe what they are experiencing because in order to be happy they need to be 'somewhere on the way to being understood and recognised'. She talks about having 'the capacity to embrace a smorgasbord of emotions. From the grand emotions of love, hate, grief, jealousy, bliss and anger, joy, to the more subtle and equally valuable states of disappointment, contentment, restlessness, boredom, ennui, longing, poignancy, hurt, frustration, tenderness and so on.' It is in allowing ourselves to feel all of these things that we learn to integrate them, and in doing so we move away from unhappiness towards contentment.[5]

We can encourage within ourselves a rigorous self-knowledge that is born of honesty and reflection. We may have some deep-seated sensitivities developed over a lifetime but perhaps particularly in childhood and early life, which can leave us wondering what is the matter with us, why we feel so undermined or out of control of our own life or reactions. There are triggers that are rooted so deeply in events and relationships from the past that we have little idea why we respond in a particular way in a particular circumstance, or even why a certain person elicits in us fear, or confusion, or a sense of being intimidated.

The feelings are very real even if the cause is buried somewhere deep in our unconscious. And they can be a significant factor in the undermining of our happiness and the insidious approach of a period of depression. If we can identify them then that is the first and very significant step in managing them so that they do not destroy us.

Memory plays a huge part in the healing process. Things that we are suppressing can chip away at our well-being without us ever being conscious of it. What is not acknowledged cannot generally be healed, so there needs to be a level of consciousness about the process. The past has to be dealt with or it can spring up when we least expect it, leaving us baffled as to why we are behaving in a certain way. Emma Forrest says of a boyfriend, 'Whilst I am working on my issues, [Simon] has buried his past, but he has buried it alive.'[6] Of course, a past buried alive is a past with the power to do damage that might not immediately be apparent but will somehow, sometime, come out.

Another useful tool is the expression of our anger. Job, in the depths of a depression with very obvious causes, laments of God:

> If I go forward, he is not there;
>   or backward, I cannot perceive him;
> on the left he hides, and I cannot behold him;
>   I turn to the right, but I cannot see him.[7]

The blank, hollow chasm of absence in which Job feels abandoned has echoes in many people's experience of depression. From the depths, Job refuses to respond to his would-be rescuers. None of the arguments of his so-called comforters, designed as they are to draw him out of his despair, hold any water so far as he is concerned. They do not touch him. He cannot relate to them. They make no sense, and do not resonate at all with his understanding of himself. In the end what happens is that he gets very, very angry with God and blurts it all out: his sense of injustice, incredulity, incomprehension, rage and devastation at the loss of all that he had, all that he loved, all that he thought were gifts from God, seemingly taken away by the same hand that bestowed them.

It is Job's rage that moves the situation on. Not that he gets any straight answers from God, but they do rebuild their relationship and there is a dialogue and some level of reconciliation. Job and God are alongside one another once again. Michael Mayne describes the relationship with brutal honesty in speaking of:

> A God who does not give simple answers to Job in his anguish . . . ;
> a God who, by his awesome gift of human freedom, cannot prevent
> the cancer cell or the Holocaust; a God who, but for one thing, would
> seem an uncaring tyrant. But it is that one thing that changes
> everything: the claim that God does not give answers. There are
> no answers. Instead, he gives himself.[8]

There is no direct explanation on God's part about why it all happened, but there is a declaration of the gratuitous and inde-structible love of the Creator for all that he has brought into being. In the end that is Job's real comfort and his means of moving on. He is able to engage with someone outside of himself once again, and the beginning of the process that leads to this new place is his unfettered expression of pure anger.

Emma Forrest writes: 'Time heals all wounds. And if it doesn't, you name them something other than wounds and agree to let them stay.'[9] Job named his wounds, loudly and clearly, and in the naming of them agreed to let them stay. We cannot expunge or ignore the damage we incur at the hands of circumstance or that we inflict on ourselves. We cannot pretend that the scars are not there, but we can live wiser, more sensitive, more awakened lives because of them.

We can also share our experiences with people whom we can trust quite simply to hold us in their love and concern. Not sharing the experience and its impact, not exploring it with others can be the difference between it being bearable or not; bearable not in the sense of easy to bear but just possible to bear without the soul caving in.

There is one more thing that I think we can do in order to fortify ourselves against depression: we can try to befriend our emptiness. Many people who suffer from depression use the language of emptiness to describe how they feel. They talk of a kind of desolation, an absence of feeling, the sense of carrying around a chasm within themselves. A common response to such an experience is to fill that gaping hole with activity, goals, company, projects and noise. The knee-jerk answer to the emptiness is to fill it.

And yet that may not be the right answer at all, or at least not the one that will ultimately stretch and energize our soul. I asked a wise friend recently, 'Why is it that in the midst of too much activity I yearn for space and stillness in my life, but run away from feelings of emptiness? Why does the idea of spaciousness feel good but the reality of emptiness feel frightening?' She recognized the conundrum from her own experience and in exploring it we observed that somehow many of us have lost our ability to be comfortable with emptiness. We have come to fear it as though it were necessarily a bad thing, rather than just a neutral space. So we flee emptiness when instead we could take the opportunity to befriend it and explore its possibilities.

In the crypt of Winchester Cathedral there is a sculpture by Antony Gormley known as Sound II. It is a lone figure, standing, slightly bending from the neck as if to see something held gently in the hands. The stone vault of the crypt ceiling provides a beautifully spacious context for the sculpture, which often stands in a sheet of still water because the crypt floods in wet weather. Gormley has said of his work generally: 'Sculpture, in stillness, can transmit what may not be seen. My work is to make bodies into vessels that both contain and occupy space. Space exists outside the door and inside the head. My work is to make a human space in space.'[10]

Surely emptiness itself does not always have to be a bad thing? Even if it is unbidden, can't it be experienced as a positive space in which to sit and wait, or think, or simply remind ourselves of the miracle of our being here at all? Of course making a conscious decision to 'befriend the emptiness' is not an easy option or even an option at all for many who suffer the sort of depression that cuts you off at the knees. If you are to work creatively with your feelings of desolation you have to have the mental energy to look at things differently, and energy is in dire supply for those who are depressed. But for those who are able to engage positively with the problem of emptiness, perhaps there is a different way of approaching that awful feeling of a chasm opening up inside, threatening to swallow our joy.

Emerging from his period of very intense fragility and recovering his sense of hope, Giles Andreae has written frankly of his experiences and begun to develop a new strand of work based on a figure called 'the Pig of Happiness'. One of the Pig's lovely wishes for us, sounding to me suspiciously like a prayer, is the one-liner, 'May you dance for ever joyful in the sweet, warm rain of life.' Well, that will not always be possible because life doesn't always rain sweet and warm. But Andreae is on to something. He says of his illness, 'I had lost any understanding of the reason to exist. But joy – our capacity to delight in one another and the world – makes sense to me now of the biggest question of all. To me, it is why we are here.'[11]

It is implicit in our understanding of a God who creates and then becomes an intimate part of that Creation that we are here to engage deeply with the embedded joy of the universe and the stunning beauty of the world and its people. Periods of depression, whether they are our own or the experience of someone close to us, disconnect our souls from that beauty and joy. Deepening our self-knowledge, finding the words to name our different emotions, getting to know what is going on inside us, knowing our triggers, unearthing memories that need to be healed, expressing our anger, naming our wounds and sharing our experiences with others – all of these things can help us towards mental good health. We can also try to befriend the emptiness and explore what might be found there, encouraging our soul to be awake to the discovery of meaning and ready to grasp the potential of emptiness to offer creative space.

9

When I grow up I want to be . . .
Is what we do what we are?

————◦•◦————

At a wedding reception many years ago my partner turned to the engaging and vivacious woman sitting next to him and asked, 'So what do you do?' 'What do I do?' she replied. 'Well, sometimes I go for a run in the early morning, I spend time with friends, I enjoy going to the cinema and I've recently begun to learn how to sew: I love it, I've just made myself a dress for the first time.' Then she paused, with a teasing smile, 'Oh, I'm sorry: did you mean what do I do when I go to work?'

It is a truism containing much truth that we often identify people by their paid employment. When someone asks, 'What do you do?' they do tend to mean in the workplace. The fact that it's one of the first things we want to know about people when we are introduced suggests that employment, particularly of the paid variety, delineates and defines people more than anything else. In fact if someone asks us, 'Who is so-and-so?' we tend to answer in terms of their job.

I have had first-hand experience of this phenomenon since giving up full-time paid employment a few years ago. In spite of having a time-consuming part-time role I'm perceived as 'not having a job' or 'not wanting a real job' by quite a lot of people. I've been asked, 'When are you going to get back in?'; 'Will you go full-time again now that the children are all at school?' (the youngest being three at the time of asking), and, in all seriousness but hilariously, when talking with someone about a colleague who had recently been promoted, 'And when are *you* going to do something interesting, Rosemary?'

Some people are happy to be known primarily by their occupation, others sit light to their 'day job' and object to being defined mainly by what they do in working hours. Still others would consider it a luxury to be able to describe themselves in terms of an interesting role, or to have a job at all. Because of our assumption that work defines us, loss of employment can leave people feeling that a part or even most of their identity has been stripped away.

There is also a sizeable proportion of people who regret that what they do with most of their time is simply not valued by society as highly as it should be: perhaps because they are retired, full-time carers or stay-at-home parents. And there are those, like the woman at the wedding, who offer a robust challenge to the idea that our paid employment should wholly define us.

When her exhibition at the Hayward Gallery opened in 2011, Tracey Emin was interviewed by John Humphrys for the *Today* programme on Radio 4. It was a really interesting exploration of the relationship between who we are and what we do; it also underlined how other people's perception of our work can fuel our decisions and our self-validation.

Emin said:

> When you get recognition and people start to understand what you're doing, or even if they don't like it but they go 'well she's been doing it for 20 years now and she's still pushing it, still pushing the boat out a bit', people tend to have more regard for you. So even if they don't like what you do they are more respectful. When people are more respectful you calm down and your chips fall off your shoulders and then you walk through the world feeling a lot happier.[1]

For Emin, her work is her art and her art is entirely tied up with herself because she is its subject matter: her body, her relationships, her thoughts and, famously, her bed and its contents. Only Tracey Emin can create Tracey Emin's art. Only she has that particular set of experiences.

Our passions and interests put each of us in an entirely unique position. None of us has the same set of circumstances, and this means two things. First, we are who we are, and no one else brings precisely the same perspective to the table. Second, we therefore have a distinctive contribution to make and if we do not make it the world misses out. So it matters very much what we 'do', what we say, what impact we have on the contexts in which we live. We undoubtedly make a difference to the individuals, organizations, communities and the friendship groups that are part of our lives. Yet there is a big leap between this idea and the assumption that 'what we do' only really counts if it is full-time and paid.

Whatever our role at work or however we spend the time that others spend in the workplace, what we do and how we go about it connects with our desire to achieve our full potential. It is part of how we seek to expand our soul. I have learnt as many lessons about myself and human nature through the absurdly wonderful life of caring for young children as I did as the associate vicar of a vibrant and wholly engaged-with-the-world central London church. As a school governor I am on a learning curve about secondary education, the needs of adolescents and the elusive nature of 'ethos'; as a trustee of an award-giving trust I am increasing in my understanding of the world of broadcasting; as a 'Thought for the Day' presenter I have briefed myself on issues as wide-ranging as alcoholism, human rights, sound bites and football. None of these activities is my official 'paid employment' and none is full-time, but each has revealed untold mysteries and inspired me to think new thoughts.

If we spend a considerable number of hours each day or week on what we might call our 'work', whether that is paid or unpaid, part- or full-time, whether it is labelled a vocation, a profession, a job or all three, it will undoubtedly shape our soul. The experiences and opportunities that it presents, the boredom, the elation and the honing of our skill sets: all of these things will have an impact on our understanding of ourselves and the world around us.

Of course for some people their work is all-consuming and does, to a great extent, define them. This can be for any number of very good reasons and is by no means always about money or status. The actress Jessica Chastain, whose profile rose considerably when two films in which she starred won their respective categories at the 2011 Cannes Film Festival, said, 'It's not about fame. It's not about money. It's about who do I get to work with, and who do I get to learn from.'[2] Or it might be about bequeathing something very particular to the world, such as a development project or a political achievement, which requires very intense and focused input over a long period of time. We need some people who are willing to sacrifice everything else for a time, perhaps even a lifetime, to achieve a project or mission that will make life significantly better for others. It may well be that this is the way some people discover the depths and breadth of themselves and truly grow their soul.

But most of us have some sense that a life outside of work is a good thing, and that if we succeed in the workplace at the expense of personal relationships or the sacrifice of other passions and ambitions we may ultimately regret not exploring the fuller depths of our souls. What many of us realize at some point is that no matter how much 'doing' we do, we won't achieve all that we want to and we won't get a sense of having finished our work or landed in the place we were aiming for, at the top of the tree, having arrived. There is almost always another rung of the ladder to climb or another achievement to notch up. A team member might want to be a team leader. A middle manager looks to senior management as the next step. If you're a CEO you could be a CEO of a bigger organization. A head teacher of a large school could be head of a more challenging school. A cabinet member could be prime minister. The prime minister could lead the party to victory more times than predecessors.

It is this realization, that the journey never ends, that inspires in some the decision to step sideways. If we have been, for a good many years, highly focused on an upward trajectory at work, it often opens a whole worm-can of nerves and jitters for our colleagues when we suddenly decide to move sideways or even step down a rung or two. The unease can be genuinely altruistic. People worry that our lives will lose momentum, that we will fail to fulfil our potential or may jeopardize our sense of self-worth if we are no longer validated by success and affirmation at work.

There are other reasons, however, that people get jumpy around those who choose to strike off elsewhere, take a different path. Sometimes the nervousness of those left behind stems from the fact that their own source of validation is being challenged: their underlying vulnerability about who they would be without their work is exposed.

I have a friend who chose to step off the ladder after 20 years within a corporate company where she was highly respected, having rapidly worked her way into a senior role at a relatively young age. Her colleagues reacted to her announcement with shock and told her that she was mad to be giving up on what she'd achieved. Some said, 'You're having a mid-life crisis. It will pass.' Of course it may be no coincidence that Debbie is in her mid 40s and making this decision. But a crisis can be a good and positive thing, an impetus to change direction. Why wait for it to go away? Why not seize the energy?

Eventually my friend's (female) boss said confidently to others, 'Don't worry, I'll take Debbie out to dinner and sort it. I know what it's all about.' Her opening lines in the restaurant ran something like this: 'I know that what you want is a baby and we'll support you however we can in that. You'll be able to come back to work as soon as you like on the same basis as now.'

Nothing was further from my (single) friend's mind than the urge to have a baby! This was not a crisis of the biological clock. It was the growing insistence of a desire to take a different turn or direction, and to stop being identified so wholly with one full-time occupation. There are many things to explore and achieve and only one life in which to pursue them. At the time of writing Debbie is still not sure what she wants to 'do' next, but she is sitting comfortably with that uncertainty, confident that the decision to do things differently has been absolutely the right one.

We all go through phases when we question the worthwhileness of how we spend our time and resources. In the first series of *Rev*, the BBC sitcom about an East End vicar, the Reverend Adam Smallbone has a crisis of faith. Very few people come to his church and he feels that the hope of the gospel is not flourishing in his local community in the way that he ought to be able to make it. The Archdeacon is flaunting his black-cab-and-sushi lifestyle while Adam is struggling to remember why he is here.

In a humorous but very poignant way the episode explores the impact on an individual who feels that he is utterly failing to make a difference. It looks fully in the face of the rage and pathos that evokes. Adam struggles with his dilemma until one evening at the end of a particularly futile day he goes to the deathbed of a woman whose husband has been trying desperately to contact him. It turns out that the woman is dying and would like the last rites. In responding to that need Adam rediscovers the fundamentals of who and what he is as a priest.

It is sometimes through 'doing' that we get our sense of self and belonging. That doing might take many forms: yours might be your volunteering, your care of a dependent relative or your paid work. Finding our identity through doing is normal. But the doing needs to be purposeful or enjoyable or both, otherwise it will not connect us with anything other than our own frustration, boredom or depression. Most of us feel the need to make a visible and quantifiable impact on the world. It is a need that grows in us for all sorts of reasons, some of which are entirely healthy. We cannot do nothing, and it is perfectly natural that we find a degree of validation in our activities. Many vital achievements and changes for the good of humanity have resulted from someone's utter commitment to their work.

For many of us, however, there are some driving forces in our lives which we might want to examine in order to ensure that in making decisions about how we spend our time we are motivated not only by what we feel we ought to do but also by what we want to do. Here I am preaching to myself, but I suspect that what I say might resonate with quite a lot of people.

Along the way I imbibed from somewhere the idea that duty and obligation should shape considerably what I do with my time. Not that this is my conscious script at all, but I don't have to delve very far below the surface of my decision-making to discover its insidious influence. When talking to people about my inability to manage my diary sufficiently to create enough space for reflection, rejuvenation or even just sleep, I am embarrassed to note how many times I use the words 'ought', 'should' and 'have to': I ought to do this because . . . I should do this as I'm obliged to . . . I have to do this, or it won't get done . . .

Duty is not a bad thing in itself. The sacrifice of personal desires is sometimes necessary for a time, for the greater good to be addressed. But if duty and sacrifice, obligation and 'oughts' are the primary drivers behind most of our decision-making they may well lead to our own deep unhappiness and a dearth of personal fulfilment. And then we need to ask ourselves, 'Who says that this is the way I "ought" to live?'

For those of us whose background has been shaped by our involvement with church, this language of duty and sacrifice is likely to be familiar. Jesus' statement that those who want to follow him must 'take up their cross' is summarily and randomly interpreted as prizing a life of sacrifice, possibly even suffering, over and above other considerations. It is sometimes said that women in particular are susceptible to the insidious demand always to put themselves last on their own list of priorities, and there is some truth in this owing to our history. However, I have seen as many men kill their more joyful and life-loving selves in the service, supposedly, of God, but actually in the service of the church.

Against this background, to frame our decisions instead with questions – such as 'Where do my energies lie?', 'What are my God-given passions?', 'When might I have a space in my diary to consider the lilies of the field?' – can be enormously liberating!

Vocation, what God calls us to be and do, is not to be equated with sacrifice, duty and a life of enervating service. Of course there will be elements of all three at times, but to me that is not the overriding meaning of the phrase 'life in all its fullness'. What we are talking about when we speak of our vocation is not just what we are called to do, but what we are called to be and to become. Our vocation is a combination of our gifts and what they suit us to, and what we get passionate about. If this is how we make decisions about what to do with our time it makes for a healthy soul.

Often we make the best contribution to anything when we *want* to make it and our gifts suit us to making it. We may have paid roles and voluntary commitments. Most of us have multiple callings. Each shapes us in different ways. We are shaped by our job, a club we belong to, an interest or passion. For each the balance will be different from the way it is for other people. But for many of us, the possibility of asking 'What do I *want* to do in this situation?' rather than 'What *should* I want or what *should* I do?' is something of a revelation and ought to be tried! It can be a struggle to start to live by this alternative mantra, but worthwhile because it opens the door to a new set of freedoms. Of course we have responsibilities, but connecting with those responsibilities via a set of oughts and shoulds can feel utterly life-sapping, and leave us in entirely the wrong frame of mind for fulfilling them. Connecting with them via passion and love can be very fruitful.

The spiritual writer Paul Coelho muses:

> I would say that [love] has to do with everything we do. First, you have to hear this call. You know, when you are close to something that justifies your life – it can be gardening, it can be cooking, it can be driving a taxi, it can be whatever you do with love – the clue is exactly that: love.[3]

The theme is, obviously, very familiar. The challenge lies in living it out without that love being frustrated by unnecessary duties and obligations.

I am not saying, of course, that we never have to do anything that does not utterly excite us or that, frankly, we would rather avoid doing. There are certain chosen priorities in our lives that lead to other responsibilities. Changing nappies is not my first love but the primary decision to have three children means that I have spent much of the past decade doing this.

Having a purpose and playing a part are a good thing and essential to human fulfilment and happiness. We seem to be wired this way. But they do not, on their own, define who we are in relation to the God who made us out of sheer gratuitous love, not because he had to or felt obliged to but because he could and wanted to. What we do and how that fulfils us and feeds those around us is negotiated in tandem with many other aspects of our lives: relationships, our belonging in the natural world, our deep-down personal contentment and flourishing, the need for space to breathe.

Victoria Coren, the writer, broadcaster and poker player, describes a version of the same thing when she tells how it can feel to succeed at something you love doing. In 2006 she won the London leg of the European Poker Tour. She says:

> I am handed the trophy, the huge heavy glass trophy that I can hardly hold. And it feels like the moment when Alice has worked out how to get her hands on the little golden key, she has bitten into the magic mushroom and grown larger and smaller and larger and smaller but finally found her balance and taken the key and unlocked the door and she finds herself at last in the beautiful garden.[4]

There is, of course, evidence to suggest that our souls grow considerably as a result of taking up an uncomfortable cross and carrying it a very long way. But this message is not mutually exclusive of the other: that God's desire for us is 'life in all its fullness'[5] and that sometimes we are just to 'be' rather than to do. Crucially, our doing will be all the more fruitful and life-giving, for ourselves and for others, if it is chosen and not forced, and chosen, at that, for the right reasons.

In the end we need the ability to sit loose to our concerns about whether we are always doing the right things with our time. As we turn to our next chapter, which tackles the question of busyness and 'too much to do', we should be mindful of the fact that we can never achieve everything, and that is absolutely fine. For there is a profound truth in the rather opaque words of Rabbi Lionel Blue's mother, as she lay dying: 'Lionel, what you've done in life you've done, and the rest is gravy.'[6]

10

Fitting the oxygen mask
Is there never time to breathe?

As I pushed a peacefully sleeping toddler around in his buggy one afternoon a passing stranger said to me, 'You'd better wake him up: life's passing him by'! It was a chance, humorous remark that left me wondering. Wondering about the human drive, which I have in more than plentiful measure, to fill every moment of our lives with wakeful activity and to limit our times of rest and recuperation for fear that we are missing out on something. Perhaps because I'm aware of the downside of that drive, I love the sight of a toddler sleeping during the daytime. Isn't that the only time in your life, other than old age, when you can sleep in the daytime with impunity, delightfully free of guilt or the sense that you should be doing something more productive?

Year after year I make the same mistake when I plant Spring bulbs in the pots on our balcony. I almost invariably put too many bulbs in one pot. When I mentioned this to a friend one day she raised an ironic eyebrow and suggested that my gardening habits might perhaps mirror the way that I live my life. Too many bulbs in one pot. Of course she's right. And although my friend kindly refrained from pointing this out, some of my plants don't flourish as well as they might, had they been given more room to take root and grow.

There's a passage in Mark's Gospel that always makes me feel sorry for Jesus. He had spent a long hard Sabbath day preaching and healing in Capernaum, dealing with the endless stream of desperate people who were brought to him. The next day, 'while it was still very dark, he got up and went out to a deserted place, and there he prayed. And Simon and his companions hunted for him.'[1] They hunted for him! I can feel my stress levels rising on Jesus' behalf. All that human need the previous day, the necessity for him to treat each person as though they were the only one, and now, having dragged himself out of bed before dawn just to get a few moments alone in prayer, he's being hunted down again.

I would hazard a guess that most of us feel hunted sometimes. There are days when you may feel that the whole town, office or family is at your door. Or that the demands of work, home, friends and extra-curricular commitments are collectively killing you. What you most want to do is flee to some protected place where you can find space and time for yourself: a retreat house, the gym, garden shed, high street or spa, depending on what lights your candle.

In the first book of Kings, chapter 19, Elijah the prophet is being hunted. He's rather brought it on himself so I don't feel the same sympathy that I do for Jesus, but it is very much the story of a desert experience. Elijah has won a contest against the prophets of Baal, therefore proving that his Lord is superior to their gods. In a rather graceless and draconian move he then has Baal's prophets killed and as a consequence flees for his own life. Out in the wilderness in a cave at the mountain of Horeb he waits for the Lord.

First there is a wind strong enough to split rocks, but the Lord isn't in the wind. Next there is an earthquake and then a fire, but neither is the Lord in those. Finally there is 'a sound of sheer silence'.[2] What a fabulous description of the all-embracing effect of utter peace and quiet: 'a sound of sheer silence'. And 'when Elijah heard it, he wrapped his face in his mantle and went out and stood at the entrance of the cave'.[3] I love that image of him wrapping his face in preparation to meet God, whose glory he could not look on directly. He takes the cloth and winds it around his head in barely suppressed anticipation of God's presence, which will emerge from the stillness after the wind, earthquake and fire.

We are, of course, all different when it comes to the quota of peace and quiet that we need in our lives. It probably depends partly on whether we are introvert or extravert, where we get our energy from and what exactly our 'reflective process' looks like. But whatever our particular requirement, we do need some opportunity to process all that happens to us and watch how our soul is responding to all the activity, events and happenings in our lives.

I once had an email from a colleague that beautifully subverted Jesus' saying, 'I came that they may have life, and have it abundantly.'[4] Catherine's message began: 'I hope you're surviving in spite of life in all its fullness.' There is, I am convinced because I have experienced it, a relentlessness that can so easily creep into our lives and steal away the joy. We're too tired to enjoy social occasions; we are rarely truly present in the room because our mind is whizzing through a mental shopping list or tomorrow's itinerary; and at work we have no chance to celebrate success or completion before moving on to the next project. This is surely not the abundance or fullness that Jesus had in mind.

Into this conversation about manic activity and overwhelming busyness, the Christian tradition offers the image of the desert as a spacious place in which we can be still and silent and attempt to find God. After his baptism Jesus famously goes out into the wilderness and prays. He is followed, centuries later, by a long line of desert mothers and fathers, all seeking something that they believe they are more likely to find 'out there', under the sweep of an uninterrupted sky, away from the glare of the city's lights, far from the demands of life as it is lived by most people.

In our attempts to connect with the God within and beyond ourselves, most of us would acknowledge the benefits of periods of silence and opportunities for space: space in the diary, space in our heads, space around us. The writer Sara Maitland made a deliberate decision to seek out significantly more silence in her life, and in doing so cleared her diary and sought out geographical landscapes that mirrored the spaciousness for which she longed. She tells us that '[Silence] is, in itself, a form of freedom; it generates freedom, free choices, inner clarity, strength. A freedom from oneself and a freedom to be oneself.'[5]

In *A Book of Silence* she recounts her experiences and reflects on the richness and adventure of the world of silence. Arguing that silence is not monotone, Maitland relates her discovery that 'The BBC's radio sound archive has tapes of a remarkable range of different silences – "night silence in an urban street"; "morning silence – dawn, the South Downs"; "Morning silence – winter moor"; "Silence – sitting room" – "garage" – "large hall" – "cement bunker" – "beach".'[6] Somehow this suggests the rich possibilities of silence and the fact that it is not about a blank emptiness, but rather framed by our experience and expectations of life. It isn't about withdrawing from the noise and hassles of everyday life for the sake of it, but for the sake of that life itself, that we may live it better on our return.

Much later in her account of her adventure, Maitland observes: 'It isn't that the brain blanks out or closes down if a person is silent, but that the electrical activity takes place elsewhere – somewhere different.'[7] As though there are untapped aspects of ourselves and human experience which we can only access once the noise of our daily lives is shut out. In turn this means that there are untapped aspects of ourselves that are not integrated into those daily lives.

There are, almost certainly, aspects of life that we simply do not engage with if we are constantly bombarded with sound and swept up in activity. But the question for most of us will not be: How can I clear all my diary commitments and delegate my responsibilities so that I can make silence my main priority for a while? Rather, it will be: how can I experience some of this in my everyday life? For most of us, most of the time, the cave and the mantle are not an option.

In order to breathe, we need to structure our lives with integral breathing space.

During the safety demonstration at the beginning of a flight there is an instruction about oxygen masks that is counter-intuitive. We are told, 'Fit your own mask before assisting children.' As I hear that, I have a pang of guilt, imagining small bewildered faces around me as I tend to my own needs while appearing to leave them to fend for themselves. But the instruction is potentially life-saving. If you yourself can't breathe you'll be in no fit state to keep anyone else alive.

My friend tells of a person she knew who was in a senior position in a very busy organization. He carried his responsibility well and seriously and yet always had time to do the other things that he wanted to do with his life. Eventually Christina asked this wonderfully rounded human being how he did it. His reply was simple. He said that because his professional role has no natural limits at all, and there is always something else that he could be doing, he has had to be rigorous in setting his boundaries and framing his own life. How obvious is that? But how seldom do we do it? Albeit that it may seem, for many, many reasons, an impossible goal, the fact is that the less of it we do, the more likely we are to come to a crashing halt at some point – probably when it is highly inconvenient!

On the same theme, Catherine, my friend who believes that 'life in all its fullness' carries a health warning, sent me a poem about ants and grasshoppers. It offers a thought-provoking contrast between people who, as a result of their extreme busyness, are pretty grumpy and distracted, always regretting the swift passing of the days, and those who manage to respond to the needs of those around them and complete the most important tasks while also finding time to relish life. The ant being the permanent grafter, the grasshopper the one with a sense of fun as well as responsibility. The poem is also an illustration, through the poet's use of humour, of the fact that when we feel swamped by life's demands, and by those we put on ourselves, a healthy dose of laughter can help to get us through.

The poem, by Barbara Dickinson, is called 'Go to the Ant' and it ends:

IS THERE A LIFE BEFORE DEATH?
wrote the grasshopper
on the lavatory wall
and added
NOT FOR ANTS[8]

One of the intriguing things about that enigmatic story of Jesus escaping up the mountain and then being hunted down is that when they found him he didn't go back with them to the town where people were waiting for him: he moved on to another place where he was equally needed. He wasn't avoiding the work. He was going with the momentum, refusing to be bogged down in one place and one set of tasks. As though he was saying, 'There is more than this group of people and this particular project. I need to frame my life, let's go.'

It's quite an energizing thought. That Jesus could say no! That he could be strategic with the use of his time. That he could do what he could do in once place, on one project, with one set of people, and then when he had achieved what he could, without waiting for anyone else to suggest that it was the right time, he could calmly make the decision to move on.

We need to frame our lives, we need to be strategic and learn how to move on to the next thing; we need space to rest and breathe, so that life in all its fullness is truly lived to the full. Yet the reality for many of us is that this fitting the oxygen mask will, at least for this phase in our lives and maybe the next too, be a case of grabbing it, taking a few deep gulps, and putting it down again in order to pick up the next task. Perhaps, if much of the activity in our lives is truly God-given and potentially life-giving, we need to find a way within rather than outside of the busyness to make room for the growth of our soul.

In a remarkable book called *Marked for Life: Prayer in the Easter Christ*, Maria Boulding offers us an alternative and very contemporary take on what it might mean to spend time in the desert. Boulding argues that there are two different sorts of desert and that either of them can offer us the challenge and the impetus to find God. The first is the sort to which we have deliberately retreated in order to find silence and space. Elijah's desert and Sara Maitland's desert. The second is the desert that is the dearth of time for ourselves, headspace and energy that result from a surfeit of activity. I had never thought of the latter as a form of desert until I read what Boulding has to say. Or at least, I had considered wall-to-wall activity to be the sort of lifestyle that God would want me to avoid by better and more judicious management of my diary and my habit of saying yes.

Boulding reminds us that classical writing on prayer, which tended to emphasize the need for time set apart and spent apart, was addressing a very different culture. It was most probably a world where silence and solitude were a little easier to come by and there were fewer distractions from prayer; whereas from birth our world subjects us to masses of information and data. She argues that God uses this in a positive way, because 'the kind of busyness that results from generosity and approachability and being fully alive can be a modern form of desert. It can be a means of self-emptying in union with Christ, a purification and a true poverty of spirit.'[9] She goes on to suggest that God says to us:

> 'Do you really think that . . . I cannot bring you into my experience of cross-bearing through asking you to live with tensions and putting on you a load of responsibilities you feel you cannot carry, or can only just carry? Or that I cannot lead you into my own experience of utter smashing failure in Gethsemane and on Calvary?'[10]

Both sorts of desert may be chosen or not. We may choose the empty sort because we recognize our need to clear space in our lives; or it may be enforced by the unwelcome solitariness of bereavement, relationship breakdown, old age, mental ill health or loss of community. There are also lots of unhealthy reasons why we might be too busy: it is easier than praying, it makes us feel important, it justifies our existence.

We can choose the desert of 'no time for myself' because we would rather live that way than face the questions that the empty desert of 'lots of time to myself' would force us up against. Or we can find ourselves in the desert of busyness just because we say yes to so many life commitments or have no choice but to accept them. What matters is that we discern well which sort of desert we ought to be in at which point in our day, week, year and life. And that this is an active decision, not just a state that we fall into.

We also need to recognize that for some of us an activity-filled life has little or no sense of 'desert' about it. It represents fruitfulness not poverty, joy rather than any sense of cross-bearing. Reading a draft of this chapter a friend of mine remarked that some of us deliberately construct a life full of activity because it feels like a good and creative thing. She said, 'I choose busyness because it makes me feel alive: can we be both busy and reflective?'

I am sure that we can. We can cultivate a way of living busily that is nevertheless characterized by a habit of asking: 'What is this about; what am I learning; where is God in this; what impact does this have on my soul?' It takes discipline and practice, but there is a difference between activity that is constant and activity that is mindless. Living mindfully is possible even in the maelstrom of passions, commitments, projects and relationships that make up many modern human lives. Tenzin Palmo, the British Buddhist nun, says,

> There are many approaches, many ways. What is unrealistic, however, is to become a mother or a businesswoman and at the same time expect to be able to do the same kind of practices designed for hermits . . . whether one is a monk, a nun, a hermit or a businesswoman, at one level it's irrelevant. The practice of being in the moment, of opening the heart, can be done wherever we are . . . It's just that it's easier to do in a conducive environment away from external and internal distractions.[11]

For those of us who fall into the 'mother or businesswoman' category or one of the many activity-focused equivalents, the salient points to take from Palmo's remarks are that there are many different ways to live a mindful and open-hearted life, consciously connecting with what is going on in the present moment and in the hearts and minds of others. It may well be easier to do this consistently away from the clamour of other people and activities, but if it is in those people and activities that we discover the sacred then to remove ourselves from all of that would be to constrain the growth of our soul rather than encourage it.

This choice, which can become for us such a dilemma, is captured beautifully in a story found in Luke's Gospel about the two sisters, Martha and Mary. Martha welcomes Jesus into her home but rushes around, distracted by all the tasks involved in hosting him and his friends. Mary, in contrast, sits at his feet and listens to his teaching. We can imagine the exasperation of the hard-pressed Martha, watching her sister in what must seem like an indulgent activity of listening to the Rabbi's teaching. But when she rebukes her sister, Jesus interjects, telling Martha that Mary has made the right choice.

It is unlikely that Jesus is advocating lack of activity or the neglect of others as a way of life. As we have seen, his days were filled just as much with meeting other people's needs as with thinking and reflecting. What seems to bother Jesus most is that Martha is 'worried and distracted by many things'.[12] His point, perhaps, is that if the activity is a distraction and an irritation to Martha's soul she needs to stop, at least until it isn't. The answer does not lie in questioning her sister's choice. She has to find her own way, the one that will most feed her soul.

So the question for you might be: Which way of life offers the best opportunity for me to live deeply and reflectively, to invigorate the life-force, the soul, the *nephesh* that makes me uniquely what I am? Am I best suited to one particular form of desert: that of silence or that of self-emptying through activity? Can I combine both? Does one work for this particular point in my life whereas in the past the other served me better and in the future things may change again? Or is the desert not my thing at all? Should I simply relish the maelstrom of busyness and the opportunities it offers to be fully alive?

A friend who was wrestling with her own questions around the purpose, meaning and direction of her life said simply and wisely, 'I either need more rest or more excitement.' The key, I think, to ensuring that we can breathe deeply lies in our ability to discern whether what we need is to look for God in the midst of activity, or to structure our lives differently in order to reduce that activity and give ourselves a clearer run at finding God in the solitude, silence and space that open up. No one can answer this question for us, though there may well be people who can listen to our questioning and reflect back what we are saying in a way that helps us to answer our own questions.

Sometimes it is helpful to explore these things with other people who are asking the same questions about the growth of their soul. We meet them in all sorts of contexts, where we might expect to do so but also in unexpected moments and encounters. We might have a very brief conversation with a stranger who inadvertently offers something that happens to resonate with our searching. We may have a friend or friends whom we know we can trust with the dilemmas that make us most vulnerable. If we are fortunate enough to have access to a church community that is asking questions that resonate with our own, this can be a source of wisdom and learning. Ultimately we need to be open to what and who we might meet in the desert of too-much-activity or the desert of silence, as well as the energizing busyness of our rich and varied lives.

When we fail to frame our lives appropriately, or when we find ourselves in the desert of 'too much to do' for the wrong reasons, it might not be God that we are running away from. In William Dalrymple's book *From the Holy Mountain* he describes an encounter with a very wise and holy man who tells him, "'God is everywhere, so you can find him everywhere." He gestured to the darkening and dunes outside: "But in the desert, in the pure clean atmosphere, in the silence – there you can find yourself."'[13]

God is everywhere and so we can discover God in the desert or in the busyness. Finding our own inner voice and presence is sometimes harder. When we say yes to the activities that revitalize our soul, frame our lives appropriately and choose our desert carefully, we ensure that we are running not only towards God, but towards the unfolding self that God is nurturing within us as we explore life's biggest questions.

11

Losing our religion . . . or not
Can the Church grow my soul?

It was a busy night in the Piccadilly branch of Strada. I was out for dinner with a friend who is also a priest. Neither of us was wearing our clerical collars: this was pleasure, not work. Ordering in Italian with a reasonable attempt at an accent, Sarah impressed the waitress, who rewarded us with a fabulous story about the pasta dish that Sarah had chosen.

'You want the *strozzapreti* – good choice. The recipe comes from a small Italian village in the mountains where the priest ate every day at the local restaurant. He was fussy about his food and always he would ask the woman who owned the trattoria for a little more of something in the pasta sauce, a little less of something else. The restaurateur continually indulged his whims until one day her patience ran out and she growled at the chef: "Bring me something that will strangle a priest." And so *strozzapreti* – strangle-a-priest-pasta – was invented.'

I don't think I'd ever seen such an embarrassed waitress as, with tears of laughter rolling down our faces, we asked her, 'You know why that's so funny? Because WE'RE BOTH PRIESTS!'

The more pompous, egotistical and self-congratulatory face of organized religion rightly draws a ferocious response from some people and a resigned sigh from others. You may have experienced a church or two that is irritating, irrelevant, out of touch with people's lives, or even destructive of individuals. Alternatively, you may have known churches that are communities of growth, nurture and inspiration. At this early stage of the discussion let me nail my colours to the mast and say that I do believe that the right church can, indeed, nurture your soul. However, there will also be church communities that are not right for you, and they come with something of a health warning.

Mark Oakley tells a story about visiting a group of 40 or so people who met on the top floor of a pub in South London.

> They all bore the scars of churchgoing in one way or another and yet didn't want to give in on the enterprise – the magnetism of mystery was still there. They wanted to share and talk about common concerns, about ethics and Christian faith and so on. But they were too angry, too hurt in lots of different ways [to do that in a traditional church]. The quality of that distilled conversation has always stayed with me and I just wish every church was full of people like that.[1]

Tobias Jones regrets that it often isn't. He is a writer, traveller and founder of a retreat community for those who are currently struggling with life. He says, 'There are few places I would take non-believers to show them why Jesus is the answer. Church, I'm afraid, is the very last.'[2]

At best, churches are communities within which the most important issues in life are opened up and explored and people are engaged in what matters most to them and to the world. Places where the quality of distilled conversation can match the one that took place in that room above a pub which had, in effect, become what a church should be.

I am what is known as a 'cradle Anglican'. My growing up was shaped by life in my dad's parish, where the congregation was our extended family and willing babysitters were never hard to find. At university I was President of the Anglican Society (what wild student days I lived), and only three years after I graduated I began training for ordination.

Given that I have known the Anglican Church from the inside all my life, it is perhaps not surprising that I love and wrestle with it in equal measure. I am inspired by the way in which some churches use sculpture, painting and architecture to challenge and grow my thoughts about God. I glory in the power of music to take me to another place, within or outside of myself, where God is. I am energized, refreshed, startled and deeply moved by things that I learn from other people who are exploring their own lives with the help of the Christian story.

I know that I am in the presence of God when I see people who are motivated by the gospel grappling with the social and political issues of our day, quite literally trying to make the world a better, more equitable and more peaceful place for others. I see Christ's love where all are honoured and affirmed irrespective of age, ethnicity, sexuality or social background. I rejoice in the opportunities that some churches offer of engagement with all of the 'big questions' that shape the content of this book. I have experienced these things in church and I love the concept of 'church' for that, because churches have embraced and challenged my soul. Although my own experience is mostly of the Church of England, I know from conversations with others that these riches are to be found in all types, sizes and denominations of church.

But the flipside to this coin is the wrestling. And again I have heard enough from others to know that my experience is shared beyond the doors of the local Church of England congregation. My friend Amy told me that she had virtually given up going to a church where she was once a regular attender, 'because there are people who recognize me yet don't bother even to say hello'. That church has an 'in crowd' and you are easily overlooked if you're not in it. Another family I know can't find a church where their children feel at home. What happens in church just does not touch them. Then there's the woman who sits in the pew resenting the fact that she has no choice but to attend, for the simple fact that her daughter won't get a place at the local secondary school if she doesn't turn up on Sundays.

My own frustrations with church are particular to my circumstances and are not triggered by every local church community, but when they trip me up they do so quite badly. This is probably because they represent, in my view, a distortion of the gospel. I don't think that I'm alone in this, and I suspect that these issues are deal-breakers for some people who are still gripped by the 'magnetism of mystery' and might otherwise happily engage with a church. I am pretty sure that those people often vote with their feet.

I have given my 'Frustrations with Church' four headings: 'Where's the Remote (God)?'; 'Uriah Heep Theology'; 'Women Need Not Apply'; and 'Jesus as a Choking Hazard'.

First, 'Where's the Remote (God)?' I am deeply frustrated by the uneven way in which some church worship describes God. We hear much of God as omnipotent, transcendent and mighty; far less of God as broken, immanent and nurturing. Expressions of Christianity that major on the God who is 'out there' touch only part of me. I need them to be balanced by affirmations of the very biblical and wonderful truth that God is 'in here', found in relationship with others and within myself. And that this is because of the Incarnation: the searing truth that God chose to be with us undefended, unprotected and vulnerable as the rest of us, in Christ.

I believe that an emphasis on divine power over and above divine intimacy has repercussions. It sets God up to fail, because in our real lived experience we do not actually detect a God who endlessly and easily fixes all that goes wrong. It gives the impression of a distant God, beyond our reach, not just mysterious but unreachable and unknowable. The Scriptures offer images of the relationship between God and humanity that evoke tenderness, openness, vulnerability and compassion, forgiveness, peace, love, negotiation and partnership. We need more of these in our worship.

There are churches that do transcendence with bells on and rather wonderfully but fail to enable in us that sense of the immanent, present God who embraces and sustains us. Yes, there is a sense in which we cannot domesticate or pin God down. Our experience of the divine will always be charged with mystery. But when there is an overemphasis on God as remote rather than God as within, this inevitably results in an impoverishment of God-at-all. Of course there are churches who tend to the opposite extreme, which can be equally unhelpful, but that is another issue!

Going hand in hand with an exclusive emphasis on a God who seems so remote as to be lost, is 'Uriah Heep Theology'. Uriah Heep is the moneylender in Charles Dickens' *David Copperfield* who is constantly telling people, 'I am very 'umble' while not actually meaning it at all. Uriah Heep theology encourages us to talk to God as though we are worms. It requires us to continually remember that 'we are not worthy'. In many Anglican churches we are asked to say, before sharing in the bread and wine, 'We are not worthy to gather up the crumbs from under your table.'[3] There are aspects of Archbishop Thomas Cranmer's legacy that I love: this, I'm afraid, is not one of them. Especially when swiftly followed by that echo of the centurion's words, 'Lord, I am not worthy to have you come under my roof, but only speak the word, and my servant will be healed.'[4]

I know what this language is trying to convey. I know my faults and they are many. I do not for a moment deny the reality of my own fallibility and my potential for being less than wholly kind, or wholly anything else that is good, all of the time. I am impatient and irritable, I sometimes shout at my children, I neglect my friends, I can be self-absorbed and I don't always make good decisions. This is just the tip of the iceberg. I have a long way to go in many areas of my life and character.

But I know all of this. Don't we all? I already beat myself up about it without being told, in church, that 'I am not worthy'. What I need to be reminded of is: You are loved and held and utterly valued. You were created in an entirely gratuitous act of freedom and joy by a God who has decided that you should reflect the divine image in yourself, and in this sense you are worthy to your very core.

What is the key message that you absorb as you sit in the pew on a Sunday morning? Is it of the grace and goodness of God and the potential that your life has if you engage with that truth and that glory? Or are you made to feel small, put firmly in your place and reminded in no uncertain terms of your shortcomings? If churches convey a distorted picture of God they inevitably give us a distorted picture of ourselves. 'God Almighty and Remote' evokes a corresponding picture of 'me-as-very-'umble'. Finding our own identity is intimately linked with finding God. You will know whether or not the worship you experience is good for the growth of your *nephesh*, your soul, the burgeoning life within you. You will know whether or not you are being nurtured.

And this brings me to my third theological bugbear: churches where 'Women Need Not Apply'. I do not necessarily mean this in the literal sense of applying for a job, though clearly that can be an issue. I mostly mean churches where the experiences and contributions of women seem to be considered marginal, tangential or even irrelevant, or are not on the radar at all.

For women, and also for men who recognize that there are aspects of the masculine and the feminine in all of us, finding our voice in the context of church can be tricky. Because it is difficult to do that in an environment that does not resonate with who we are. In describing her own faith journey, the Anglican priest Lucy Reid talks about the experience of training at theological college in England at a time when it was taken for granted that God is male and priests are male. She knew that there was something missing, something not right about this. She was unable to articulate what that was until in the pages of the Scriptures she discovered feminine metaphors for God that connected her in a new way with the divine.

In the first chapter of her remarkable book *She Changes Everything*, Reid explores that biblical imagery of God as midwife and womb, and God as Sophia, Wisdom. She looks at the feminine words used for God in the Hebrew language, and at the idea of

God as mother, used frequently in the early Church and later by the medieval mystics. She explores how in some times and cultures Jesus' mother Mary has been seen as the feminine face of God. Describing her own response when she discovered all of these rich traditions, now largely ignored in church liturgy, she writes, 'Perhaps most fundamentally of all, I felt recognition of a God who could look like me.'[5]

How could it be to sit in a pew and not have to filter out the language that excludes us? How might it feel to have the usual range of images used to describe God extended to include midwife, fierce and protective mother, nurturer and protector, figure of Wisdom alongside God at the Creation of the world? How freeing it might be to get a glimpse of a God who upturns our expectations and connects with the feminine aspects of our soul. How much more whole does the Trinity feel when somewhere in among those three figures of Father, Son and Holy Spirit the avowedly feminine aspects of God break through.

In the early 1980s when the Church of England still did not ordain women at all, Reid and her husband, who had trained at theological college alongside her, moved to Canada in order that she might be ordained priest. Her experience of being unable to explore fully her sense of vocation and, crucially, her sense of self, precipitated a decision to go elsewhere in order that she could begin to do that.

It is a decision that I understand. On occasions I find myself ashamed and embarrassed to talk to my daughters about what the Anglican Church does to women. In October 2011 they came with us to the enthronement of a new bishop and I asked them after the service: 'Did you realize how amazing it is that the dean of that cathedral was a woman and so was the Archbishop's representative?'

'What's so amazing about that?' one of them asked.

I took a deep breath and began to explain that it's only since 1987 that the Church of England has ordained women as deacons, and since 1994 that we've been allowed to be priests. I could hardly bear to tell her that we still can't be bishops: sometimes you just want to leave your daughters in delightful innocence about such things. But I did tell her, because it won't help her to shield her from reality, and unfortunately the reality is that currently the Church of England, the church I have loved and wrestled with in equal measure since childhood, refuses to open up an entire formative area of its life to the influence, gifts and experience of women, thereby placing a question mark over the validity of the ministry of every woman priest and over what it means to be a woman at all.

Where 'Women Need Not Apply' it is questionable whether souls can fully thrive and that includes the souls of men. We need the depth and breadth of inspiration that can be learned from those who are different from ourselves as well as from those who share our perspectives and background. The theologian Trevor Dennis writes:

> I cannot read as a woman, nor write as a woman, because I am a man. I cannot cross the border into their territory. All I can do is come to the boundary fence and listen, attempt to learn, and then on my side of it attempt to apply what they have taught me.[6]

Enabling this listening and providing a safe space in which people can meet at the boundary fence of their different experiences seems to me to be one of the fundamental tasks of the Church and a deeply fertile way in which to feed our soul.

So finally we come to Jesus. Some years ago I sent a present to my cousin's little girl for her first Christmas. It was a variation of a Russian *matryoshka* doll: one figure inside another inside another. The theme of this particular set of dolls was the Nativity: the largest was a wise man, then came a shepherd, then Mary, then a tiny, tiny baby Jesus. Aware that this was not an age-appropriate gift for a 7-month-old child and intending it to be treasured over the years rather than played with immediately, I added a cautionary message: 'Please note that Jesus is a potential choking hazard.'

Unfortunately I suspect that some people may agree, having been put off churches by Christians who have a too-sure monopoly on Jesus. 'Jesus as a Choking Hazard' is my final frustration with some parts of the Church. I emphasize the 'some parts' because there are churches that succeed in engaging people in an honest and exciting exploration of who Jesus might be, and might even prompt and sustain that excitement in teenagers. But then there are churches that clearly feel they own Jesus, and pretty much always know the answer to that slightly Sunday school question: 'What would Jesus do?'

How do we access the Jesus who will make us think, not cringe, who will draw us towards him, not cause us to duck; who has a message that we might really want to hear and wrestle with and embrace; who could help us to unearth some insights about life as it really is and some suggestions as to how to live with it? The Jesus who might excite, inspire and expand our soul?

There is an episode in Barbara Kingsolver's novel *The Poisonwood Bible* when the missionary who is the main protagonist in the story falls victim to the Western culture that he has been attempting to force upon his African hearers. Having heard enough about this character, 'Jesus', whom the missionary wants them to accept as Lord and Saviour, the villagers decide, wholly outside their usual custom, to have a democratic vote on whether or not they will do so. In the end Jesus loses, 11 to 56.[7] And I cannot help thinking that he might have been rather amused. Jesus becomes a choking hazard if we try to force in others a particular response to what and who he might be.

The task of the Church is to lead people towards Christ and provide the encouragement and resources for them to explore him for themselves. In his wonderful poem 'St Joseph', Tom Ward evokes the sheer miracle of Jesus' beginnings and his cosmic significance alongside the enticing idea that we can explore this person for ourselves. Joseph is planning their first journey as a new young family, when Mary comes to him with an invitation.

St Joseph

'That's how she found me, fretting over fares
and calculating distances. And when I blushed she smiled,
while one brown toe grew careless in the dust,
scuffing up the road I'd sketched between Beth Horon
    and the sea.

We were alone then, no shepherds or kings to fill
the distances between us. Just I who agree to host
the mess and fury of this birth, and she
who consents to host the rest: the Holy, Complex,
Still, Uncharted One who bent the shallow sky convex
to touch her flesh, just once, in Galilee.

Joseph, she said, her flexing toe still wrinkling the earth,
Joseph he's yours as well you know.
Come and see him.[8]

How we experience and respond to the Jesus of the Gospels will depend on myriad different variables and perspectives in our own lives. But one thing of which we can be sure is that no one has the monopoly on who or what he was and is, and if they think they do, he tends to become a choking hazard rather than the bread of life.

Some time ago our son Joseph, two years old at the time, had been clattering noisily up and down the hallway with his trains and cars when he suddenly went ominously quiet for a little too long. I found him in the bathroom with the Johnson's baby shampoo bottle upturned, pouring the beautiful yellow liquid all over the floor and glorying in what he'd released.

I know it's a slightly odd connection to make but he reminded me a little of the woman in the Gospels with her jar of pure nard, who for a moment escaped the usual constraints of orderly and seemly behaviour and, like a child, did what it was obvious to her had to be done. She smashed the bottle and poured out its aromatic contents over the head of the one person in the room who knew what it was about, who knew the meaning at the heart of her reckless and passionate gesture.[9]

We break things open to see what's inside, we make connections, we discover a new layer of meaning in the world and in our lives. Churches need to be places within which we can do this with confidence, and witness others doing the same. If you have found a church like that, whatever its other challenges might be, you should consider sticking with it. Allow it to help you break things open and discover what is at the heart of everything.

In the many places where churches enable people to come and explore the big questions in life, that is a very good thing. Church can undoubtedly nurture and excite souls. If you are looking for a church that will enlarge your soul, find one where people are regularly reminded that they are made in the image of God: a little tarnished perhaps, yet still beautiful. Find one that enables you to connect with 'God within' as well as 'God out there'. Find one that seeks actively to embrace and learn from the experience of all human beings, female and male. Find one that helpfully accompanies people as they explore the significance of Jesus and the Gospels, and will remind you that 'he's yours as well', as it teaches you ways to deepen your relationship with Christ.

If you are reading this and thinking how easy it is to be choosy about church if you live in a city within travelling distance of several options, but that where you live the church is part of a group, is only open once a month, and wouldn't recognize much of what I've described above, I don't underestimate your dilemma. The distinctive approach of Anglicanism is for every local church to serve its own community and therefore your presence in your local church is invaluable to those others who worship there. But if that community is unable to recognize your perspectives and contribution there does come a time when there is little choice but to travel further afield to find the nurturing community that you long for. If that isn't an option then there are virtual churches and Christian communities and resources online which you might want to explore before you give up on the idea of church altogether.

Church can nourish and nurture our soul, can refresh our take on God, can offer us insights and point us to places where God is at work in the world. It can instil in us a love of learning about life and reassure us that we are an integral part of God's picture and God's plan. It can 'big up' our souls, provided that we find a place within it that is determinedly and courageously opening up the big questions. Provided that we can find a safe and energizing space in which they might be rigorously and honestly explored.

12

The gift of 'just because'
Does my life have a point?

This book has explored some of the pressing issues that shape our soul. The way we respond to those insistent and nagging questions will determine the colour and shape, the music and the texture, the flavour and character of our life. If we feed and nurture our *nephesh*, the life force that fuses our inner and outer worlds, it will grow. Our soul will look big in everything, because it is free, expansive, lively, generous, at ease with itself and poised for what comes next. If we starve and constrain our *nephesh* it may falter and fail.

I have tried to tease out a number of interwoven issues, all of which influence our outer and inner lives: how we might respond creatively to life's stages and transitions, learning both self-acceptance and the courage to sit loose to ourselves; how we might sit comfortably, offer our particular perspective and find our distinctive voice; the influence of other people on our emerging identity, regardless of whether we are someone who sits on the margins of groups or enjoys being at the centre of the crowd; our soul's relationship with the places we have known, the pilgrimages we have made and our sense of home; our desire to find patterns and correlations in our experience of creation and our global community; the gift, to ourselves and others, of our fragility, and the space that can open up for our soul's growth when we are prepared to be appropriately naked before others.

I have looked at the elusive nature of happiness and the need for us to address what is difficult in ourselves in order to grow in contentment; our brushes with depression, whether our own or other people's, and what they say about meaning and emptiness; the need to embrace the activities that invigorate our *nephesh* while being wary of life-sapping 'oughts'; finding a mechanism for taking a deep breath that best suits our own very individual soul; and risking an encounter with institutional religion in the hope that we may find there some resources to address the big questions.

In all of this I have not sought to give definitive answers but to offer stories and sign-posts that might prompt you to a deeper understanding of the questions. It occurs to me that there is one final question that overarches the others and needs some attention: 'Does my life have a point?' I have framed it as though asked by an individual, because we each experience it in the context of our own hearts, minds and lived experience as particular human beings. But of course there is a more cosmic version that asks, 'Does life have a point at all?' You might have asked yourself either of those questions because you have been through a period of feeling lost, purposeless and lonely. Or they may have arisen for you because suddenly you have sensed the precarious nature of all that we have, the fact that what we have been given can so easily be taken away.

If we take all of the other big questions seriously we will find meaning and connection in our lives. We will experience a sense of fulfilment for various reasons at different stages. But we might still be left with a residual itch to know whether there is any overarching purpose in any of it.

In his wonderfully titled book *Straight to the Pointlessness*, Mark Hart writes:

> God freely gives us life. He does not need to and gets nothing from it for himself. He has not made us to be useful for his own needs nor for any other purpose beyond the universe. Much as we may like to justify our existence, or achieve something which establishes our right to live, we cannot do so and need not do so ... If we ask what is the ultimate point of the life we create together, the answer must be that there isn't one, or that this life is its own point. And that is not a disappointment – it is our freedom. It is God's freedom, shared with us.[1]

The central argument of Hart's book is that our point lies not in what we do or say. Our point lies in the fact that we just are: that is it. We are, each one of us, a unique creation to be wondered at and rejoiced in. A gift to the world with no strings attached. God creates not out of a sense of purpose and certainly not from obligation, but because it is in God's nature to do so. Creation is a spilling over, a limitless sharing of the life of God: out of that supreme gratuitousness we come into being.[2] You might have sensed this giftedness in occasional moments of deep contentment, when one of your life's dreams is taking shape after a long wait. Or in the experience of the sort of comfortable companionship that comes with lifelong friendship. It's a feeling of being gently but firmly held, a sense that each new day is a privilege to be gloried in. It is a sudden but profound experience of 'just because-ness'.

We are just because we are. But this is not to say that it does not matter what we do with our lives or that there is no reason to do anything at all. Yet the purpose and the doing are not necessary to justify our existence. We have no obligation to God: God does not engage with the language of obligation or have any 'parental expectations' of us at all. How much easier should that make it for us to luxuriate in life, how much more relaxed can we be, how much more natural is the process of growing our soul if we are able to grasp, hold on to and live by the truth: that we are; we wonderfully are; just because we are; just because God is. How much heartache will be avoided, how much justification and obligation circumvented, if we can really believe that our worth lies not in anything that we do or say or achieve or acquire, but in the sheer miracle of our being at all.

What might it look like, this life lived in a spirit of questioning and the experience of freedom? What are we freed from and what are we freed for? At the Winter Olympics in 2010 two sports commentators were talking about the female silver medal winner in that strangely named event, the moguls. They said that her technique was flawless but her style was somehow too constrained and technically rigid to win her the race. One of them commented, 'Perfect very rarely wins you the gold medal. It has to be free.'

You might know this truth from either end. You may have experienced moments in your life that were by one definition perfect but somehow, and you're not sure why, fell short of being wonderful experiences. A surprising number of happily married people look back on their wedding day with that sense of 'perfect but not enjoyed to the full'. Or you may know the truth of freedom that is in no sense perfection and is all the more enjoyable for that. Perhaps you have frittered away an afternoon on a messy but enjoyable task that has little point beyond the immediate enjoyment of the participants: cooking an inept but enjoyable meal with housemates, creating a leaky dam of toppling stones in a river. Freedom and flaws can be much more fun than the sterile dotting of 'i's and crossing of 't's.

I have long suspected that God is much more interested in the idea of freedom than flawlessness and that the point of our life is not about striving to tick every box and kick the ball neatly into the back of every goal in sight. Perfection may be appropriate in some areas of life but not in the living of life as a whole, not in respect of the big picture. That big picture is continually growing, evolving and becoming, and if we worry a lot about the finishing touches too much of our energy will be diverted away from simply exploring and relishing each experience. You will probably know people whose obsession with flawlessness makes them very difficult to be with. It neither brings the best out in them nor in those around them. The sheer, unconstrained freedom of just being often has so much more to offer.

In John's Gospel there is a disturbing and very significant crunch moment when Jesus is presented with a woman caught in adultery. The religious leaders want to catch Jesus out, so they effectively ask, 'What is this woman's fate?' They know that Jesus will want to respect the law but that he will not want the woman to die. They think they have put him in an impossible situation and that he will condemn either himself or the woman with his reply.

Jesus, having listened to the question, bends down and writes with his finger on the ground.[3]

When I was a child I had an illustrated Bible with a picture in it of that very moment: the moment when Jesus stooped and wrote in the dust. It was such a frustration to me that in that picture it wasn't possible to see what Jesus was writing. What was the point of the story, if we didn't get to see the magic words? I think I thought that whatever they were, those words would unlock 'the secret'. Precisely what secret, I'm not sure, but something that would transform everything and help me to understand God and the world so much better.

That story lodged in my heart and my imagination through childhood, adolescence and young adulthood into middle age, because it hints that in Jesus are to be found the answers to the trickiest questions of life. The hope that Jesus reflects and reveals what life and God are all about is a hope that is still very much alive in me – though I've stopped thinking that I just need to know what he wrote on the ground in order to understand everything.

Of course there isn't an answer written in the dust. Christ offers us no formula whereby we might live our lives without making any major mistakes or taking any wrong turnings. There is no blueprint which, if followed rigidly, will bring the right results deep in our very souls. Wholeness does not come that way. It comes through Jesus just being there, alongside us, bending down, writing in the dust, straightening up and looking us in the eye, telling us how he feels about us and then sending us out to live life to the fullness of our capacity.

Wholeness comes through a relationship with the God who is always within and alongside us, making something new. We bring the whole of ourselves before God and ask: what do you want me to do with this bit, or that bit, because it's become part of me and I need to move on from it and I don't know how? And here God is, looking up from the dust to say, 'Has no one condemned you. Then neither do I. Go your way, and from now on do not sin again.' God sets us free in our weakest and most fragile moments.

Even in our sin. He says, 'Stop sinning, move on, know that you are loved.'

What God offers us is something much more risky and free-form than a blueprint or a formula for living life well. He offers a relationship, established in the words, 'Neither do I condemn you.' Then he sends us out not on our own, but in him, who will draw out of us what is best. From the pages of the Scriptures we get stories, pictures, parables and insights that are essential to our understanding of the God to whom we relate. Yet it's the relationship that will lead us on, give us the confidence to be open to new experiences, to say goodbye to the rubbish in our lives, to be remade afresh. We nurture this relationship by paying attention to it by whatever means our lives offer. You will grow closer to the God who nurtures, heals and forgives through your relationships with those people whom you nurture, heal and forgive. You will flex your 'courage muscle' each time you try something new and discover in doing so that you can make mistakes and survive, even flourish.

In 2010 our then 8-year-old and 5-year-old daughters decided to run the London Mile in aid of Sport Relief. Their enthusiasm was not in doubt. Their excitement was infectious. Their focus was impressive. But they had never run a mile without stopping before, never entered a nationally organized race even of such a friendly and non-competitive nature, and in the end I have no doubt that it was their relationship with their patient and long-suffering father, who ran alongside them, that got them to the finish line. The courage that we need is the courage to be fully ourselves, radiant with God's glory, filled with God's purpose, ready when God calls us to follow, however tricky it gets. Belonging in God should feel like this. It should carry the sense of being accepted exactly as we are, and being sent on our way to live life well. This relationship in itself invests our life with meaning.

In an article by Lionel Shriver in the *Guardian Online* I came across a metaphor for our relationship with God. Shriver describes how it feels to share a bed with another human being, the sheer luxury of just being together, enwrapped, dozing in and out of sleep:

> You are each other's geometric destiny. You feel at once protective and protecting. It is like holding yourself . . . The time does not simply vanish. It passes – sumptuous, languorous and thick. Sleep is the very opposite of death. Your experience of being and only being is at its most intense.[4]

There is something in Shriver's description of just dozing, existing and simply being with someone that speaks into our ideas about not needing to justify our existence, simply luxuriating in being bodily, alive, here, in the now, with no need for anything else. The sheer sense that on one level, at least, nothing else matters.

There are many other experiences in life that have the potential to remind us of the gloriously unfettered gift of our 'just because-ness', of our ultimate, unquestionable worth. These are ways in which our life here and now reminds us that we are, in the sheer miracle of our existence, amazing. Our exploration of 'flow' (Chapter 7), the state of being wholly and attentively in the present and fully engaged with what we are doing, resonates here. When we are in the zone and experiencing flow we are experiencing what it feels like simply to be – and to be wonderful, and to know that our being and wonderfulness both come from the God who delights in our very existence.

If we are an artist, it might be our creativity that triggers this response of glorying in the simple and miraculous fact of our being; perhaps particularly in the moment when we create something unique and beautiful, entirely of ourselves and entirely other than ourselves. Or it might be the world of ideas that awakens us to the wonder of the human mind, and our mind, particularly as we explore an intellectual field that enthuses and fires us. It may be an occasion spent with friends we have known for many years and with whom we can simply relax and kick back, time that flies by as we relish being together and all that we enjoy in one another as the clock goes unheeded. I can sit down at my laptop and write for several hours, only stopping to boil the kettle occasionally. If the writing goes well, when I eventually stop I have a sudden instant of feeling fantastic, like a wonderful adrenaline rush of well-being.

We will all have our equivalents, depending on what most gives us life, and they somehow align us with the core of our being and that of the world, a sense of meaning and being and rejoicing that lies at the heart of what it means to be a fully alive human being. It connects with the sheer sense of being where you belong. In the right place: the place that is home. I think that may be what it feels like to belong in God.

So the idea is that we are gloriously pointless, in the best sense of the word, unfettered by the need to justify ourselves, simply engaged in becoming what we are meant to be. This does not of course mean that nothing we do matters. Everything that we do has an impact on the growth of our soul or the well-being and health of others, or both. We don't exist in isolation but in relationship. And in all our relating we make a difference. In William P. Young's novel *The Shack*, the character who represents God says to the protagonist:

> Mack, if anything matters then everything matters. Because you are important, everything you do is important. Every time you forgive, the universe changes; every time you reach out and touch a heart or a life, the world changes; with every kindness and service, seen and unseen, my purposes are accomplished and nothing will ever be the same again.[5]

We should not be surprised that we have such amazing potential to change things for the better: we are made in the image of God. A common understanding of the biblical myth that we know as the Fall is that when Adam and Eve ate of the fruit that they had been forbidden, the image of God in human beings was utterly destroyed. Yet there is a rabbinic tradition[6] that argues that we did not lose the *image* of God but simply some of the lustre, the polish, the gleam, perhaps the glory. The image of God in humanity has not been erased: it is still there, ready to be polished up once again![7] We might need a bit of polishing, but we are, essentially, who we are meant to be. Our souls are continually learning, experiencing and unfolding, and we are becoming more ourselves all of the time.

We could say that this is the point and purpose of our lives. But it is not a goal towards which to strive or a means to justify ourselves: we just do it because it is a natural process, essentially leading us to become more fully what we are already. The way that we engage with the biggest questions in life will determine whether we starve the life of our soul, burying it or building a protective shell that serves only to deprive it of light, or whether we nourish and foster our *nephesh*, encouraging it to expand so that it grows from strength to strength. Yet this should never be an arduous task or yet another project that we feel constantly under pressure to deliver.

Again from *The Shack*:

> what God has given us is the ability to respond, to respond freely in every given situation. Not a set of responsibilities to live up to, which would inevitably become a yardstick against which we and others measured ourselves, and failed.[8]

If you are someone who tries to justify your existence by targets ticked off, learning objectives met, goals achieved, certificates ranged on the walls of your life, there is something of a shift in perspective required. Not that those things are worthless in themselves: far from it. But they do not define our own worth. Perhaps we should get into the habit of embracing the miracle of just being, of just enjoying, of 'just because'.

With the reassurance that 'we are, just because' and that what we are is rather wonderful, our *nephesh*, the life force within us, is poised to grow and expand, to reflect more fully the glory of being fully human and fully in God's image. It is open to learn from life's joy, complexity and nuance, and from opportunities for both doing and reflecting. As we negotiate life's stages and transitions, learning what to take with us and what to leave behind, we understand that the questions will always be with us – shaping our enquiry, pointing us in new directions, interweaving themselves with our daily lives, encouraging us to look deeply into all things. And we know that because we both love the questions and wrestle with them they have the potential to grow our souls, making them gracious, resonant, sensitive, vital and gloriously expansive. So that when occasionally we dare to risk the question, 'Does my soul look big in this?', the answer, with a smile, will be a resounding 'YES'.

Notes

Introduction

1 For an exploration of the word *nephesh*, see Paula Gooder, *Heaven*, London: SPCK, 2011, p. 80.

2 Richard Rohr, 'A future for men', *Third Way*, vol. 33, no. 7, September 2010, p. 18.

3 Andrew Shanks, *Anglicanism Reimagined: An Honest Church?*, London: SPCK, 2010, p. 2.

1 The John Lewis stages of life

1 For example, see Viv Groskop, 'A word on our sponsors: John Lewis – Always a Woman', *The Guardian*, 26 April 2010.

2 Mark 1.12–13.

3 Matthew 4.1–11; Luke 4.1–13.

4 Pema Chödrön, *Start Where You Are*, London: HarperCollins, 2005, p. 65.

5 Chödrön, *Start Where You Are*, pp. 29–30.

6 Emma Cook, 'How to manage a change of heart,' *Psychologies*, November 2011, p. 82.

7 Michael Symmons Roberts, 'Anatomy of a perfect dive', in *Corpus*, London: Jonathan Cape, 2004, pp. 67–72. Reproduced by kind permission of the poet and Jonathan Cape.

8 Caitlin Moran, *How to Be a Woman*, London: Ebury Press, 2011, pp. 224–5.

9 Neil LaBute, *In a Forest Dark and Deep*, world premiere, Vaudeville Theatre, London, 2011.

10 Andy Burnham MP, interviewed by Roy McCloughry, *Third Way*, vol. 43 no. 5, June 2011, p. 20.

2 Comfortable in my own skin

1 Elif Shafak, *Black Milk: On Motherhood, Writing and the Harem Within*, New York: Viking, 2011.

2 Elif Shafak, interviewed by Jo Carruthers, *Third Way*, vol. 34, no. 6, July–August 2011, p. 18.

3 John Rodwell, interviewed by Terence Handley MacMath, *Church Times*, 14 August 2009.

4 Judges 4.5.

5 Philippians 3.8.

6 Paraphrase and précis of Philippians 3.8b–12, based on NRSV translation.

7 Deuteronomy 33.27.

8 Pete Ward, 'The red carpet to salvation', *Third Way*, vol. 34, no. 2, March 2011, p. 13.

3 The school playground

1 Andy Burnham MP, interviewed by Roy McCloughry, *Third Way*, vol. 43, no. 5, June 2011, p. 18.

2 Esther 4.14.

3 Kerry Kidd, 'Amazons or earthmothers?', *Third Way*, vol. 34, no. 3, April 2011, p. 12.

4 John Rodwell, interviewed by Terence Handley MacMath, *Church Times*, 14 August 2009.

5 1 Corinthians 13.11–12.

6 Anne Michaels, *Fugitive Pieces*, London: Bloomsbury, 2009, p. 14.

4 Born in the North

1 Jacqui Marson, 'How can I put my past behind me?', *Psychologies*, May 2011.

2 Emma Forrest, *Your Voice in My Head*, London: Bloomsbury, 2011, p. 43.

3 Genesis 28.17.

4 Genesis 28.19.

5 Genesis 32.30.

6 John Pritchard, *God Lost and Found*, London: SPCK, 2011, p. 90.

7 Genesis 12.1.

8 Adam Weymouth, 'In sacred footsteps', *Third Way*, vol. 34, no. 3, April 2011, p. 29.

9 Andrew Rumsey, *Strangely Warmed: Reflections on God, Life and Bric-a-Brac*, London: Continuum, 2010, p. 112.

5 This gossamer web

1 Matthew 10.30.
2 Andrew Rumsey, *Strangely Warmed: Reflections on God, Life and Bric-a-Brac*, London: Continuum, 2010, p. 96.
3 Rumsey, *Strangely Warmed*, p. 84.
4 Barbara Brown Taylor, *Leaving Church: A Memoir of Faith*, New York: HarperCollins, 2007, p. 23.
5 John 3.2.
6 John 3.6–12.
7 Roald Dahl, *The Minpins*, London: Puffin, 2008, p. 48.
8 Don Paterson, 'Why do you stay up so late?', in *Rain*, London: Faber and Faber, 2009, p. 9. Reproduced by permission.
9 Michael Perham, *To Tell Afresh*, London: SPCK, 2010, p. 92.
10 Mark Oakley, St Paul's Forum Debate, 'Happiness', held at St Paul's Cathedral, 26 October 2010, video available on the Cathedral website.

6 Down the stairs backwards

1 A reference to Richard Rohr, *Falling Upward: A Spirituality for the Two Halves of Life*, San Francisco: Jossey-Bass, 2011, p. xxx.
2 Pema Chödrön, *Start Where You Are*, London: HarperCollins, 2005, p. 33.
3 Michael Mayne, *Pray, Love, Remember*, London: Darton, Longman and Todd, 1998, p. 56.
4 John 19.25.
5 See Luke 24.13–32 for the full story.
6 Victoria Coren, 'Me, my dad, and the deal of a lifetime', *The Observer Review*, 13 September 2009, extract from *For Richer, For Poorer: A Love Affair with Poker*, London: Canongate, 2009.
7 Lucy Winkett, *Our Sound is Our Wound: Contemplative Listening to a Noisy World*, London: Continuum, 2010, pp. 95–6.
8 Mike Riddell, *Sacred Journey: Spiritual Wisdom for Times of Transition*, London: SPCK, 2010, p. 79.
9 Emma Forrest, *Your Voice in My Head*, London: Bloomsbury, 2011, p. 105.
10 For full details, see <www.brart.org>.

7 'Never fully known, never properly kissed'

1 Martin Seligman, *Authentic Happiness: Using the New Positive Psychology to Realize Your Potential for Lasting Fulfillment*, London: Nicholas Brealey Publishing, 2003.

2 Martin Seligman, *Flourish: A Visionary New Understanding of Happiness and Wellbeing – and How to Achieve Them*, London: Nicholas Brealey Publishing, 2011.

3 Seligman, *Flourish*, p. 11.

4 Jemima Kiss, 'How I kicked my digital obsession – and rediscovered the joys of the real world', *The Observer*, 24 April 2011.

5 Mark Oakley, St Paul's Forum Debate, 'Happiness', held at St Paul's Cathedral, 26 October 2010, video available on the Cathedral website.

6 Mark Oakley, 'Happiness' debate.

7 Mark Williamson, quoted in 'The meaning of success', *Edition* (John Lewis Magazine), issue 8, p. 58.

8 Luke 6.20–26.

9 Michael Mayne, *Pray, Love, Remember*, London: Darton, Longman and Todd, 1998, p. 45, quoting Stendhal, in turn quoted by Anita Brookner in a lecture on the painter Jacques Louis David.

8 The rawness of peeled carrots

1 Giles Andreae, 'How depression left best-selling author shaking, sobbing and unable to get out of bed', *Mail Online*, 22 March 2010.

2 Richard Rohr, 'A future for men', *Third Way*, vol. 33, no. 7, September 2010, p. 18.

3 Mark 5.21–43; Matthew 9.18–26; Luke 8.40–56.

4 Luke 8.44–46.

5 Susie Orbach, St Paul's Forum Debate, 'Happiness', held at St Paul's Cathedral, 26 October 2010, video available on the Cathedral website.

6 Emma Forrest, *Your Voice in My Head*, London: Bloomsbury, 2011, p. 84.

7 Job 23.8–9.

8 Michael Mayne, *Pray, Love, Remember*, London: Darton, Longman and Todd, 1998, p. 49.

9 Forrest, *Your Voice in My Head*, p. 166.

10 Antony Gormley, 1995, taken from Tate St Ives, 'Antony Gormley – some of the facts', notes for teachers, 16 June to 2 September 2001.

11 Giles Andreae, 'Purple Ronnie creator on depression', *Times Online*, 28 November 2009.

9 When I grow up I want to be . . .

1 Tracey Emin talking to John Humphrys, *Today*, BBC Radio 4, 16 May 2011.

2 Quoted by Andrew Gumbel in 'Who's Jessica Chastain?', *The Observer*, 5 June 2011.

3 Paulo Coelho, interviewed by Brian Draper in *Third Way*, vol. 33, no. 5, June 2010, p. 16.

4 Victoria Coren, 'Me, my dad, and the deal of a lifetime', *The Observer Review*, 13 September 2009, extract from *For Richer, For Poorer: A Love Affair with Poker*, London: Canongate, 2009.

5 John 10.10, GNB.

6 Lionel Blue quoting his mother in an interview with Stephen Moss, Saturday Interview, *The Guardian*, 13 November 2010, p. 39.

10 Fitting the oxygen mask

1 Mark 1.35–36.

2 1 Kings 19.12b.

3 1 Kings 19.13.

4 John 10.10.

5 Sara Maitland, *A Book of Silence: A Journey in Search of the Pleasures and Powers of Silence*, London: Granta, 2009, p. 221.

6 Maitland, *A Book of Silence*, p. 186.

7 Maitland, *A Book of Silence*, p. 280.

8 Barbara Dickinson, 'Go to the Ant'. Reproduced in *Rags of Time*, under the auspices of The Society of Civil Service Authors: Poetry Workshop, 1991. Permission to reproduce sought.

9 Maria Boulding, *Marked for Life: Prayer in the Easter Christ*, London: SPCK, 2010, pp. 13–14.

10 Boulding, *Marked for Life*, p. 14.

11 Tenzin Palmo, quoted by Sara Maitland, *A Book of Silence*, p. 273.

12 Luke 10.41.

13 William Dalrymple, *From the Holy Mountain*, London: HarperCollins, 1997, p. 410, quoted in Maitland, *A Book of Silence*, p. 219.

11 Losing our religion . . . or not

1 Mark Oakley, St Paul's Forum Debate, 'Happiness', held at St Paul's Cathedral, 26 October 2010, video available on the Cathedral website.

2 Tobias Jones, 'Living in rhythm', *Church Times*, 25 March 2011.

3 Holy Communion Service, The Book of Common Prayer, 1666. Extracts from The Book of Common Prayer, the rights in which are vested in the Crown, are reproduced by permission of the Crown's Patentee, Cambridge University Press.

4 Matthew 8.8 and the Mass of the Roman Rite.

5 Lucy Reid, *She Changes Everything: Seeking the Divine on a Feminist Path*, New York: T&T Clark, 2005, p. 21.

6 Trevor Dennis, *Sarah Laughed: Women's Voices in the Old Testament*, London: SPCK, 2010, p. 3.

7 Barbara Kingsolver, *The Poisonwood Bible*, London: Faber and Faber, 2000, p. 380.

8 Tom Ward, 'St Joseph', *Third Way*, vol. 33, no. 10, December 2010, p. 46. Reproduced by kind permission of the poet.

9 Mark 14.3; Matthew 26.7.

12 The gift of 'just because'

1 Mark Hart, *Straight to the Pointlessness: A Christian Account of Life and the Universe*, London: Continuum, 2011, pp. 3, 4–5.

2 Hart, *Straight to the Pointlessness*, particularly Chapter 1.

3 John 7.51—8.8.

4 Lionel Shriver and Jenni Murray, 'Sleep apart, stay together', *Guardian Online*, 16 April 2011.

5 William Paul Young, *The Shack*, London: Hodder and Stoughton, 2007, p. 235.

6 Genesis Rabbah 12.6.

7 Paula Gooder, 'Being priestly, being female', presentation to the Annual Conference of the National Association of Diocesan Advisers in Women's Ministry, June 2011.

8 Young, *The Shack*, p. 205.

Bibliography

Books

Maria Boulding, *Marked for Life: Prayer in the Easter Christ*, London: SPCK, 2010.

Barbara Brown Taylor, *Leaving Church: A Memoir of Faith*, New York: HarperCollins, 2007.

Pema Chödrön, *Start Where You Are*, London: HarperCollins, 2005.

Roald Dahl, *The Minpins*, London: Puffin, 2008.

Trevor Dennis, *Sarah Laughed: Women's Voices in the Old Testament*, London: SPCK, 2010, first published 1994.

Emma Forrest, *Your Voice in My Head*, London: Bloomsbury, 2011.

Paula Gooder, *Heaven*, London: SPCK, 2011.

Mark Hart, *Straight to the Pointlessness: A Christian Account of Life and the Universe*, London: Continuum, 2011.

Barbara Kingsolver, *The Poisonwood Bible*, London: Faber and Faber, 2000, first published 1998.

Sara Maitland, *A Book of Silence: A Journey in Search of the Pleasures and Powers of Silence*, London: Granta, 2009.

Michael Mayne, *Pray, Love, Remember*, London: Darton, Longman and Todd, 1998.

Anne Michaels, *Fugitive Pieces*, London: Bloomsbury, 2009, first published 1997.

Caitlin Moran, *How to Be a Woman*, London: Ebury Press, 2011.

Michael Perham, *To Tell Afresh*, London: SPCK, 2010.

John Pritchard, *God Lost and Found*, London: SPCK, 2011.

Lucy Reid, *She Changes Everything: Seeking the Divine on a Feminist Path*, New York: T&T Clark, 2005.

Mike Riddell, *Sacred Journey: Spiritual Wisdom for Times of Transition*, London: SPCK, 2010.

Richard Rohr, *Falling Upward: A Spirituality for the Two Halves of Life*, San Francisco: Jossey-Bass, 2011.

Andrew Rumsey, *Strangely Warmed: Reflections on God, Life and Bric-a-Brac*, London: Continuum, 2010.

Martin Seligman, *Authentic Happiness: Using the New Positive Psychology to Realize Your Potential for Lasting Fulfillment*, London: Nicholas Brealey Publishing, 2003.

Martin Seligman, *Flourish: A Visionary New Understanding of Happiness and Wellbeing – and How to Achieve Them*, London: Nicholas Brealey Publishing, 2011.

Elif Shafak, *Black Milk: On Motherhood, Writing and the Harem Within*, New York: Viking, 2011.

Andrew Shanks, *Anglicanism Reimagined: An Honest Church?*, London: SPCK, 2010.

Lucy Winkett, *Our Sound is Our Wound: Contemplative Listening to a Noisy World*, London: Continuum, 2010.

William Paul Young, *The Shack*, London: Hodder and Stoughton, 2007.

Poetry

Barbara Dickinson, 'Go to the Ant'. Reproduced in *Rags of Time*, under the auspices of The Society of Civil Service Authors: Poetry Workshop, 1991.

Don Paterson, 'Why do you stay up so late?' in *Rain*, London: Faber and Faber, 2009.

Michael Symmons Roberts, 'Anatomy of a perfect dive' in *Corpus*, London: Jonathan Cape, 2004.

Tom Ward, 'St Joseph', *Third Way*, vol. 33, December 2010.

Articles

Andy Burnham MP, interviewed by Roy McCloughry, *Third Way*, vol. 43, no. 5, June 2011.

Paulo Coelho, interviewed by Brian Draper, *Third Way*, vol. 33, no. 5, June 2010.

Victoria Coren, 'Me, my dad, and the deal of a lifetime', *The Observer Review*, 13 September 2009, extract from *For Richer, For Poorer: A Love Affair with Poker*, Canongate, 2009.

Andrew Gumbel in 'Who's Jessica Chastain?', *The Observer*, 5 June 2011.

Tobias Jones, 'Living in rhythm', *Church Times*, 25 March 2011.

Kerry Kidd, 'Amazons or earthmothers?', *Third Way*, vol. 34, no. 3, April 2011.

Jemima Kiss, 'How I kicked my digital obsession – and rediscovered the joys of the real world', *The Observer*, 24 April 2011.

Jacqui Marson, 'How can I put my past behind me?', *Psychologies*, May 2011.

Stephen Moss, interviewing Rabbi Lionel Blue, Saturday Interview, *The Guardian*, 13 November 2010.

John Rodwell, interviewed by Terence Handley MacMath, *Church Times*, 14 August 2009.

Richard Rohr, 'A future for men', *Third Way*, vol. 33, no. 7, September 2010.

Elif Shafak, interviewed by Jo Carruthers, *Third Way*, vol. 34, no. 6, July–August 2011.

Tate St Ives, 'Antony Gormley – some of the facts', notes for teachers, 16 June to 2 September 2001.

Pete Ward, 'The red carpet to salvation', *Third Way*, vol. 34, no. 2, March 2011.

Adam Weymouth, 'In sacred footsteps', *Third Way*, vol. 34, no. 3, April 2011.

Mark Williamson, quoted in 'The meaning of success', *Edition* (John Lewis Magazine), issue 8.

Online

Giles Andreae, 'How depression left best-selling author shaking, sobbing and unable to get out of bed', *Mail Online*, 22 March 2010.

Giles Andreae, 'Purple Ronnie creator on depression', *Times Online*, 28 November 2009.

Emma Cook, 'How to manage a change of heart,' *Psychologies*, November 2011.

Tracey Emin, talking to John Humphrys, *Today*, BBC Radio 4, 16 May 2011.

Viv Groskop, 'A word on our sponsors: John Lewis – Always a Woman', *The Guardian*, 26 April, 2010.

Mark Oakley, St Paul's Forum Debate, 'Happiness', held at St Paul's Cathedral, 26 October 2010, video available on the Cathedral website.

Lionel Shriver and Jenni Murray, 'Sleep apart, stay together', *Guardian Online*, 16 April 2011.

Lectures

Paula Gooder, 'Being priestly, being female', presentation to the Annual Conference of the National Association of Diocesan Advisers in Women's Ministry, June 2011.

Theatre

Neil LaBute, *In a Forest Dark and Deep*, world premiere, Vaudeville Theatre, London, 2011.